A.A. Castor

Pathways to Self

Exploring Spirituality Without Divine Figures

Table of Contents

Pathways to Self: Exploring Spirituality Without Divine Figures

A.A. Castor

Dedication

To my beloved family,

Your unconditional love, unwavering support, and endless encouragement have been my greatest blessings. From the earliest days of dreaming to the challenging moments of writing, you have stood by me with patience and belief. This book is as much yours as it is mine, a reflection of the values you've instilled and the faith you've shown in me. Thank you for being my rock and my inspiration.

To my dear friends,

Your friendship has illuminated my path with laughter, shared moments, and invaluable support. You've cheered me on through every triumph and lifted me up through every challenge. Your belief in my endeavors has been a source of strength and motivation. This book is a testament to the power of friendship, and I am grateful for each of you who has walked this journey by my side.

To God,

Your grace and guidance have been my constant companions. In moments of doubt, you've shown me the way; in moments of joy, you've multiplied my gratitude. This book is a testament to your faithfulness and the blessings you've bestowed upon me. May it serve as a reflection of your love and the lessons you continue to teach me.

With heartfelt gratitude and love,

A.A. Castor

Copyright © 2024 by A.A. Castor

All rights reserved. No part of this book may be reproduced, stored in a retrieval system, or transmitted in any form or by any means—electronic, mechanical, photocopy, recording, scanning, or otherwise—except as permitted under Section 107 or 108 of the 1976 United States Copyright Act, without the prior written permission of the publisher, except for brief quotations embodied in critical reviews and certain other noncommercial uses permitted by copyright law.

For permission requests, contact A.A. Castor at:

Address: Urban Deca Home Metro Manila, 1230

Email: dev.castortony@gmail.com

Website: www.tonyc.info[1]

This book is a work of non-fiction. Names, characters, places, and incidents are either the product of the author's research or are used factually. Any resemblance to actual persons, living or dead, events, or locales is entirely coincidental.

Printed in Philippines

Philippine Copyright Law:

The Intellectual Property Code of the Philippines (Republic Act No. 8293) provides protection to literary and artistic works from the moment of their creation. It includes provisions for the rights of authors and copyright owners, including the exclusive right to reproduce, distribute, perform, and display their works. Unauthorized use or reproduction of copyrighted materials is subject to legal penalties under this law.

---

1.   http://www.tonyc.info

Why I Am Writing This Book

The motivation behind writing this book stems from a growing awareness that many people today are searching for a meaningful way to engage with spirituality that doesn't necessarily involve belief in a god or adherence to traditional religious structures. In a world that is becoming increasingly secular, globalized, and focused on individual autonomy, more people are turning inward to explore their own paths toward fulfillment, inner peace, and personal growth. This book aims to explore that shift and offer practical guidance for those seeking to deepen their spiritual lives without relying on divine figures.

In recent years, I've seen a profound transformation in how spirituality is understood and practiced. There's been a clear movement away from external, theistic models of spirituality toward more personal, self-directed approaches. People are now embracing practices like mindfulness, meditation, and self-reflection, not as religious rituals, but as ways to foster emotional healing, inner peace, and self-awareness. This evolution is fascinating because it allows for a more individualized and flexible experience of spirituality—one that is deeply personal, yet also connected to universal human experiences such as the search for meaning, purpose, and connection.

My purpose in writing this book is to give voice to this shift and offer a guide for those who are on a similar journey. I wanted to provide a resource that acknowledges the growing number of people who seek spiritual fulfillment but don't necessarily find it in conventional religious settings. By focusing on self-discovery, emotional healing, and ethical living, this book serves as a roadmap for anyone looking to build a spiritual practice rooted in personal growth and inner peace.

At its core, this book is about empowering individuals to take ownership of their own spiritual journey. The ideas and practices explored here are meant to help readers develop a deeper understanding of themselves, heal emotional wounds, and cultivate a sense of meaning that is grounded in their personal values and experiences. I believe that spirituality should be accessible to everyone, regardless of their belief in a higher power, and this book is written with that in mind.

Additionally, I wrote this book to challenge the assumption that spirituality is inherently tied to religion or divine beings. For many, the concept of spirituality extends far beyond the framework of organized religion—it's about cultivating mindfulness, living ethically, and striving for personal growth. By exploring these themes, I hope to encourage readers to see spirituality as a practice of self-empowerment, emotional healing, and compassionate living, rather than something that requires adherence to external dogma.

In writing this book, I also wanted to create a space where individuals can reflect on their own journeys and find practices that resonate with them. Spirituality, in my view, is not a one-size-fits-all approach. It's deeply personal and can take many forms depending on each person's unique experiences and desires. My hope is that this book serves as a companion for those navigating the complexities of modern life, offering insights and tools that help them lead more intentional, peaceful, and fulfilling lives.

Ultimately, I wrote this book because I believe that spirituality is a vital part of the human experience, even in a world where traditional religious structures are losing their influence. Whether through mindfulness, self-compassion, or ethical living, there are countless ways to cultivate a rich, meaningful spiritual life without the need for divine figures. This book is my contribution to that conversation, and I hope it helps readers connect with their true selves and find greater peace, purpose, and balance in their lives.

Warning and Disclaimer

The information and practices shared in this book are intended to serve as a guide for those seeking to explore spirituality without reliance on divine figures. The content is designed to offer insights, tools, and exercises for personal growth, mindfulness, and emotional well-being. However, the advice and recommendations provided in this book are not meant to substitute for professional medical, psychological, or therapeutic care.

While self-focused spiritual practices can be beneficial for many individuals, it's important to recognize that personal growth, emotional healing, and mindfulness are deeply personal experiences. The results of these practices may vary from person to person. Readers are encouraged to use discretion and adapt the practices to suit their individual needs, circumstances, and emotional health. If you are experiencing severe emotional distress, trauma, or mental health challenges, it is strongly advised that you seek support from a licensed professional such as a therapist, counselor, or medical practitioner.

The exercises, suggestions, and practices outlined in this book are based on general approaches to self-awareness, self-care, and ethical living. They are not prescriptive in nature and are meant to be used as starting points for exploration. The author and publisher are not responsible for any specific outcomes or consequences resulting from the application of the information contained in this book.

This book is not affiliated with any religious organization or spiritual authority. It does not claim to represent or replace any formal spiritual or religious teachings. The content is based on the author's research, observations, and personal perspectives, and is meant for educational and personal development purposes only.

Readers are encouraged to consult with a professional if they have questions or concerns about their emotional, physical, or spiritual well-being. Any actions taken by the reader based on the information provided in this book are done so at the reader's own risk.

By reading this book, the reader agrees that the author and publisher shall not be held liable for any damages, harm, or negative consequences that may result from following the suggestions or practices outlined.

About the Author

A .A. Castor is a dedicated writer and researcher with a passion for exploring the intersections of spirituality, personal development, and social philosophy. With a background in studying human behavior, religious history, and cultural evolution, Castor's work often focuses on how individuals can cultivate a deeper sense of meaning, purpose, and connection in their lives without the need for traditional religious structures. His writing seeks to empower readers by offering practical tools and insights that foster emotional healing, self-awareness, and personal growth.

Castor's interest in non-theistic spiritual practices grew out of a personal exploration of mindfulness, meditation, and self-compassion. Recognizing that many people today are searching for ways to enrich their inner lives outside the confines of organized religion, he began researching and writing about the numerous paths available for cultivating spiritual well-being rooted in the self. His work delves into the ways that modern life, with its complexities and pressures, has led many individuals to seek a more personal, self-directed approach to spirituality—one that prioritizes inner growth, emotional balance, and ethical living.

In addition to his writing, Castor is an active podcaster and educator, where he discusses topics such as leadership, history, social dynamics, and the role of spirituality in navigating the challenges of contemporary life. Through his podcasts and other media, he encourages listeners to reflect on their own experiences, embrace personal responsibility, and find empowerment in crafting their own spiritual journeys.

Castor's work is deeply informed by a belief that personal growth and emotional healing are essential to living a fulfilling and purposeful life. By blending practical guidance with philosophical inquiry, his writing aims to provide readers with the tools they need to lead more mindful, intentional, and spiritually connected lives.

When not writing or podcasting, Castor enjoys researching historical figures and philosophical movements that have shaped human thought, often seeking to draw lessons from the past to apply to the challenges of the modern world. He is committed to creating accessible, thoughtful content that helps individuals explore the depths of their own potential and live with greater clarity, balance, and inner peace.

For more about A.A. Castor's work, you can visit his website or listen to his podcast, which focuses on leadership, history, and the evolving nature of spirituality in today's society.

Introduction: The Rise of Self-Centered Spirituality

In a world increasingly defined by scientific discovery, social change, and individualism, traditional religious practices centered around gods and divine figures are being reevaluated. More than ever, people are searching for spiritual fulfillment in ways that don't require belief in a higher power. They are looking inward, focusing on self-awareness, personal growth, and ethical living to find meaning and purpose in their lives. This shift toward spirituality that emphasizes the self, rather than worship of the divine, has opened new avenues for understanding how one can live a meaningful and spiritually enriched life.

Spirituality without divine figures challenges the long-held belief that faith must involve the worship of a god or adherence to religious doctrine. It proposes that enlightenment, fulfillment, and ethical living can be achieved through self-exploration, discipline, and personal reflection. From ancient traditions like Buddhism and Jainism to modern movements like veganism and secular humanism, people are discovering that spiritual practices rooted in personal responsibility and inner peace can be just as profound as those based on divine worship.

The purpose of this exploration is to offer a deep dive into the various spiritual paths that prioritize the self. These paths encourage individuals to take control of their spiritual development, relying not on divine intervention but on personal growth, ethical choices, and inner harmony. By examining diverse traditions and philosophies, this book sheds light on how non-theistic spiritual practices help individuals cultivate meaningful and purposeful lives.

This subject matters today more than ever. As modern life becomes increasingly fast-paced, interconnected, and secular, the desire for spiritual fulfillment remains strong. However, many are turning away from theistic frameworks in favor of practices that align with their personal experiences and beliefs. Secularism, mental health awareness, and ethical living have all contributed to the rise of non-theistic spirituality, providing individuals with alternative ways to connect with their inner selves and the world around them. This book aims to explore these paths, offering insight into how spirituality without gods is shaping the spiritual landscape of the 21st century.

Overview of the Concept: What Does Spirituality Without Divine Figures Mean?

SPIRITUALITY WITHOUT divine figures refers to the pursuit of meaning, purpose, inner peace, and moral development without the reliance on a god, gods, or supernatural beings. It is a form of spirituality that focuses on the individual's inner life, self-awareness, and ethical living rather than worship, prayer, or belief in a higher power. This concept emphasizes personal responsibility for spiritual growth and fulfillment, often rooted in practices like mindfulness, meditation, ethical living, and philosophical contemplation.

At its core, this approach to spirituality suggests that enlightenment, moral guidance, and life purpose can emerge from within, rather than being granted by an external deity or following religious dogma. People who follow this path believe that the answers to life's most profound questions—such as the meaning of existence, the nature of happiness, and the path to inner peace—are discovered through personal reflection, self-discipline, and ethical actions rather than divine revelation.

Key Elements of Spirituality Without Divine Figures:

1. **Self-Realization**: A central theme is the belief that each person has the capacity to realize their own truth, purpose, and enlightenment. Spiritual growth becomes a journey inward, where the individual reflects on their actions, thoughts, and beliefs to better understand themselves and the world.

2. **Ethical Living**: In the absence of divine commandments, moral and ethical frameworks are often developed based on reason, compassion, and personal responsibility. Traditions like Buddhism and Jainism, for example, advocate for non-violence, kindness, and respect for all living beings, with the

motivation coming from the desire to reduce suffering and promote well-being, rather than to please a higher power.

3. **Mindfulness and Meditation**: Practices such as mindfulness and meditation are commonly used in non-theistic spiritual paths. These techniques help individuals cultivate awareness of their thoughts, emotions, and actions, allowing them to gain deeper insights into their nature and develop a sense of peace and clarity without needing to look toward a deity.

4. **Inner Peace and Fulfillment**: Rather than seeking fulfillment through divine intervention or prayer, this kind of spirituality encourages individuals to find peace within themselves. By mastering emotions, understanding desires, and controlling impulses, individuals can achieve a sense of contentment and purpose in life that does not depend on external supernatural forces.

5. **Connection to the World and Others**: While non-theistic spirituality does not rely on divine figures, it often emphasizes the interconnectedness of all life. People may focus on their relationships with others, the environment, and their place in the universe. Practices such as veganism or ethical humanism reflect the idea that spirituality is not about divine worship, but about fostering compassion, responsibility, and respect toward all living beings.

Why It Matters

In today's increasingly secular world, many people are seeking spiritual fulfillment outside of organized religion. Some may be disillusioned with religious institutions or simply find that belief in a god does not resonate with their understanding of the world. For others, the focus on personal empowerment, ethical living, and inner peace is more appealing than traditional religious practices.

Spirituality without divine figures provides an alternative path for those who still seek meaning, purpose, and connection in life but prefer to do so through self-exploration and personal responsibility. It challenges the traditional notion that spirituality must be tied to the worship of a god, offering instead a framework that celebrates the power of the individual to achieve spiritual growth and fulfillment on their own terms.

This concept is gaining traction as more people look inward for answers and prioritize practices that promote mental, emotional, and ethical well-being. By exploring this topic, your book will address a growing desire to find meaning in life outside of divine narratives, offering readers a way to cultivate a rich, meaningful spiritual practice focused on the self rather than the supernatural.

Purpose of the Book: Exploring the Different Spiritual Paths That Focus on the Self Rather Than a God or Gods

THE PRIMARY PURPOSE of **"Pathways to Self: Exploring Spirituality Without Divine Figures"** is to offer readers a comprehensive guide to various spiritual traditions and philosophies that center on the self rather than on the worship or belief in a god or gods. It aims to shed light on the idea that spiritual fulfillment, ethical living, and personal growth can be achieved without reliance on divine beings, opening up a deeper understanding of how individuals can find meaning and purpose within themselves.

This book seeks to:

1. Expand the Understanding of Spirituality

Traditional definitions of spirituality often involve belief in a higher power or a god. This book will challenge that notion by introducing readers to a variety of spiritual paths that emphasize the self as the source of wisdom, peace, and ethical guidance. It aims to broaden the definition of spirituality, demonstrating that it is possible to live a deeply spiritual life rooted in personal experience, inner exploration, and self-awareness.

Readers will discover that spirituality is not confined to religious belief systems, but can also be found in secular or philosophical practices such as Buddhism, Stoicism, and even modern movements like veganism. This expanded view of spirituality encourages readers to embrace diverse ways of nurturing their inner lives, regardless of their religious background.

2. Showcase Diverse Spiritual Paths

The book will explore various spiritual traditions and practices that focus on the self rather than on deities. By presenting a range of belief systems—from ancient practices like Buddhism and Jainism to modern movements like secular humanism and veganism—the book will offer readers insights into how different cultures and philosophies have approached the question of spiritual growth through self-awareness and personal responsibility.

This exploration will show that while these paths may differ in their specific practices, they share common themes such as ethical living, personal empowerment, mindfulness, and self-discovery. By comparing and contrasting these paths, the book will provide readers with a toolkit of spiritual practices that they can apply to their own lives, regardless of their personal beliefs about the existence of a god.

3. Provide Practical Guidance for Personal Growth

One of the key objectives of the book is to equip readers with practical tools and techniques to cultivate their spiritual well-being without relying on divine intervention. Practices such as meditation, mindfulness, ethical living, and self-discipline will be presented as ways to achieve personal growth, inner peace, and emotional balance.

Readers will find that the journey to self-fulfillment requires discipline and introspection but offers a profound sense of empowerment. By focusing on self-responsibility, the book will help readers build their own spiritual practices based on their values, goals, and experiences. Whether someone is new to spirituality or looking for an alternative to religious traditions, this book will offer them practical steps for living a spiritually meaningful life.

4. Address Modern Spiritual Needs

As society becomes increasingly secular, many people are searching for meaning and purpose outside of traditional religious structures. This book aims to address the spiritual needs of modern readers who are interested in cultivating a sense of purpose, inner peace, and ethical responsibility without subscribing to a particular faith or religious doctrine.

By offering a non-theistic approach to spirituality, **"Pathways to Self"** will resonate with readers who are seeking alternatives to religion, while still acknowledging the human need for connection, growth, and purpose. It will provide a spiritual framework that is flexible, inclusive, and adaptable to the diverse needs of today's readers, showing that fulfillment can come from within rather than from an external divine source.

5. Promote Self-Empowerment

At the heart of this book is the idea that individuals have the power to shape their own spiritual journey. By focusing on self-mastery, personal growth, and ethical living, the book will empower readers to take control of their spiritual development without relying on traditional religious authorities or belief systems.

The message of self-empowerment is particularly important for those who may feel disconnected from or disillusioned by organized religion. The book will show that spiritual fulfillment is not something that needs to be bestowed upon an individual by a higher power, but rather something that can be achieved through intentional action, reflection, and self-awareness.

This focus on personal empowerment aligns with modern values of autonomy and self-reliance, making the book relevant to readers who prioritize individuality and self-discovery in their spiritual practices.

6. Foster Ethical and Compassionate Living

The book will also emphasize the role of ethical living in spiritual development. Many of the spiritual traditions explored in this book, such as Buddhism, Jainism, and veganism, place a strong emphasis on compassion, non-violence, and responsibility toward others. By highlighting these ethical dimensions, the book will show readers that living a spiritually rich life also involves being mindful of one's impact on the world.

Through these examples, readers will learn how to align their personal values with their spiritual practices, fostering a deeper sense of connection to both themselves and the world around them. The book will encourage readers to lead lives that are not only spiritually fulfilling but also ethical and compassionate.

7. Offer a Roadmap for a Fulfilled Life Without Divine Belief

Ultimately, the purpose of the book is to provide a roadmap for readers who are seeking to lead spiritually meaningful lives without the need for belief in a god or gods. By exploring different paths that prioritize self-awareness, ethical living, and personal growth, the book will help readers navigate their spiritual journeys with clarity and purpose.

This roadmap is especially valuable for those who may have felt lost or unfulfilled within traditional religious frameworks. The book will offer them a new way to approach spirituality that is grounded in the self, providing them with the tools they need to find meaning, peace, and fulfillment on their own terms.

Why This Subject Matters Today: How Modern Life and Thought Lead People to Seek Spirituality in Non-Theistic Ways

IN TODAY'S RAPIDLY evolving world, traditional religious structures and beliefs are being questioned, challenged, and, in some cases, abandoned. The pace of modern life, coupled with the rise of scientific understanding, individualism, and social change, has led many people to seek spirituality in ways that don't rely on theistic frameworks. **"Pathways to Self: Exploring Spirituality Without Divine Figures"** is a timely response to these shifts, offering insight into why an increasing number of people are drawn to non-theistic spiritual practices.

1. The Decline of Traditional Religious Belief

Over the past few decades, there has been a marked decline in adherence to organized religion, particularly in Western societies. People are increasingly identifying as "spiritual but not religious" or rejecting formal religious affiliations altogether. Studies show a rise in secularism and agnosticism, especially among younger generations, who are questioning the role of religion in a scientifically driven, pluralistic society.

This decline in traditional religious belief has opened the door to new forms of spiritual exploration. While many may no longer believe in a god or follow a specific religious doctrine, the desire for meaning, purpose, and connection remains strong. Non-theistic spiritual practices offer a way for people to engage in self-reflection, ethical living, and personal growth without adhering to religious institutions or divine worship.

2. The Search for Meaning in a Secular World

In a world where materialism, technology, and rapid change often dominate, many people feel a sense of disconnection or emptiness. The pressures of modern life, including work stress, social isolation, and the constant bombardment of information, can leave individuals feeling lost or spiritually unfulfilled. Traditional religious answers may seem insufficient or outdated for addressing these contemporary issues.

Non-theistic spiritual practices, such as mindfulness, meditation, and ethical living, provide an alternative path to finding meaning and fulfillment. They allow individuals to cultivate inner peace, resilience, and self-awareness in a world that often feels chaotic and disconnected. By focusing on personal growth and self-discovery, these practices offer a sense of grounding and purpose without relying on religious dogma.

3. The Rise of Individualism and Personal Responsibility

Modern thought increasingly values individualism, autonomy, and personal responsibility. In contrast to religious systems that prescribe belief in a higher power and communal worship, non-theistic spiritual practices emphasize the power of the individual to shape their own life and find their own meaning. People are drawn to the idea of being in control of their spiritual journey, free from external authority or religious institutions.

In a time when many people seek to define their identity and beliefs on their own terms, non-theistic spirituality offers the freedom to explore inner truths without needing to conform to a predefined religious narrative. This aligns with the modern emphasis on self-empowerment and personal development, where individuals are encouraged to take responsibility for their own spiritual growth, ethics, and well-being.

4. The Integration of Science and Spirituality

Another reason non-theistic spirituality is gaining popularity today is the increasing intersection between science and spiritual practices. As science explains more about the nature of the universe, the mind, and the human condition, many find it difficult to reconcile traditional religious teachings with scientific understanding. Concepts like evolution, cosmology, and neuroscience have challenged the validity of divine creation stories and religious explanations of existence.

However, science and spirituality are not necessarily at odds. Practices such as meditation and mindfulness have been scientifically proven to benefit mental and physical health, offering a bridge between secular knowledge and spiritual practice. By focusing on the self, mindfulness, and ethical behavior, non-theistic spiritual traditions align well with a scientifically oriented worldview. This allows people to embrace spirituality in a way that is compatible with rational, evidence-based thinking.

5. The Emphasis on Mental Health and Well-Being

Mental health and well-being have become significant priorities in modern life. As people seek to balance their emotional, psychological, and physical health, non-theistic spiritual practices provide valuable tools for self-care and inner peace. Meditation, yoga, and mindfulness, for example, are widely used to reduce stress, improve mental clarity, and cultivate emotional resilience. These practices don't require belief in a deity, making them accessible to individuals from all walks of life.

As the conversation around mental health grows, spirituality is increasingly being recognized as an essential aspect of holistic well-being. Non-theistic practices focus on nurturing the self, cultivating self-awareness, and building inner strength—elements that are critical to maintaining mental health in an often stressful, fast-paced world. For many, these practices offer a spiritually fulfilling alternative to traditional religious rituals, helping them to achieve balance, peace, and purpose in their lives.

6. Globalization and Access to Diverse Philosophies

In the age of globalization, people have greater access to a variety of spiritual traditions from around the world. Ancient Eastern philosophies like Buddhism, Jainism, and Stoicism have gained popularity in the West, offering non-theistic approaches to spirituality that focus on self-mastery, mindfulness, and ethical living. The internet, travel, and cultural exchange have made it easier for individuals to explore and adopt practices that resonate with them, regardless of their geographic or cultural origins.

The spread of these ideas has contributed to the rise of non-theistic spiritual paths that prioritize inner peace, self-discipline, and compassion. With more exposure to different spiritual traditions, individuals are empowered to curate their own spiritual experiences, borrowing from a range of philosophies and practices that align with their values. This flexibility appeals to those who seek a personalized, self-directed approach to spirituality.

7. Ethical Living and Global Responsibility

As awareness of global challenges such as climate change, animal rights, and social justice increases, many people are seeking spiritual frameworks that align with their ethical concerns. Non-theistic spiritual practices, such as veganism and environmental mindfulness, offer a way to live ethically without invoking religious commandments or divine judgment. These practices emphasize compassion, non-violence, and responsibility toward the planet and other living beings.

In a world that increasingly values social and environmental responsibility, non-theistic spiritual paths provide a moral compass based on empathy, rational thought, and a commitment to reducing harm. For many, this is a more appealing and practical approach to ethical living than traditional religious rules, which may not fully address modern global issues.

Conclusion: The Growing Relevance of Non-Theistic Spirituality

In today's world, people are searching for spiritual fulfillment in ways that reflect modern values, scientific understanding, and a desire for personal autonomy. **"Pathways to Self: Exploring Spirituality Without Divine Figures"** is an essential exploration of how non-theistic spiritual practices offer meaningful alternatives to traditional religious belief systems. By focusing on self-awareness, ethical living, and inner peace, these paths meet the needs of a contemporary audience seeking purpose and fulfillment in a rapidly changing world.

This subject matters today because it addresses the evolving spiritual needs of individuals who are navigating life in a secular, globalized, and often overwhelming environment. It offers a way for people to find spiritual depth, meaning, and well-being without reliance on divine figures, while encouraging personal responsibility and ethical engagement with the world.

Chapter 1: The Concept of the Self in Spiritual Traditions

Throughout history, the concept of spirituality has been closely linked to the worship of gods and divine figures. In many cultures, spiritual growth was seen as something bestowed upon individuals by external powers, be they gods, spirits, or universal forces. However, across time and place, certain traditions have taken a different approach, placing the focus not on divine intervention but on the individual self. In these traditions, the self is viewed as the center of spiritual development—both the seeker and the source of enlightenment, wisdom, and moral authority.

Understanding the self in a spiritual context requires an exploration of how different traditions define the individual in relation to the universe, life's purpose, and the pursuit of inner peace. In contrast to theistic belief systems that position humans as dependent on divine guidance or grace, these philosophies emphasize that the answers to life's deepest questions lie within the individual. The self is seen as both the starting point and the ultimate destination on the spiritual journey.

Over time, this shift—from a divine-centric to a self-centric spiritual framework—has gained prominence in both ancient and modern philosophies. Practices like meditation, mindfulness, and ethical self-reflection have replaced prayer and divine worship as the primary tools for achieving inner peace and personal growth. This chapter explores how different spiritual traditions, from Buddhism to secular humanism, have embraced the self as the key to spiritual fulfillment and examines the philosophical evolution that has led to this focus on personal responsibility and inner mastery.

By redefining spirituality as something that comes from within rather than from above, these traditions offer a new way of thinking about the nature of existence, purpose, and ethical living. They challenge the idea that external forces are necessary for spiritual growth, encouraging individuals to look inward for the wisdom, strength, and insight needed to navigate life's challenges.

Defining the self in spiritual contexts

THE CONCEPT OF THE self has long been a focal point in various spiritual traditions, serving as the key to understanding one's place in the world, the nature of existence, and the path to fulfillment. In spiritual contexts, the self is often more than just the individual personality or ego—it is seen as the essence of a person, the innermost being that connects one to deeper truths, both about the self and the universe.

In theistic religions, the self is frequently defined in relation to a divine figure. One's spiritual journey may revolve around understanding their relationship with a god, surrendering to divine will, or seeking salvation through a connection with a higher power. However, in non-theistic spiritual traditions, the focus shifts inward. The self is not a reflection of divine will but a source of wisdom, growth, and enlightenment in its own right. Here, the journey is about unlocking the self's potential, cultivating awareness, and achieving balance or liberation through personal effort and understanding.

The self, in this context, becomes a vessel for spiritual exploration. It is viewed as the seat of consciousness, emotions, desires, and thoughts, all of which need to be understood and mastered to reach spiritual fulfillment. In practices such as meditation and mindfulness, the goal is to observe and understand the self without judgment, recognizing its patterns, desires, and attachments in order to transcend them. The self is also seen as the creator of meaning in non-theistic spirituality. Without reliance on divine commands or external salvation, individuals must forge their own path to meaning through personal experience, reflection, and ethical action.

In Buddhism, for example, the self is not considered an eternal, unchanging entity but rather a collection of experiences, thoughts, and feelings that are constantly in flux. The goal is to transcend attachment to this fluid self and to reach a state of non-attachment and enlightenment. In Stoicism, the self is seen as the master of one's emotions and actions, with spiritual growth coming through self-discipline and rationality. In secular humanism, the self is the source of morality and ethical living, emphasizing that each individual has the capacity for reason, empathy, and the pursuit of a meaningful life without divine guidance.

Thus, in these non-theistic traditions, the self is not merely the starting point of the spiritual journey—it is the journey itself. It becomes the object of contemplation, transformation, and liberation. Understanding and mastering the self allows individuals to unlock their potential, achieve inner peace, and engage with the world in a more profound, intentional way. It is through this lens that the self is viewed as the core of spiritual life, providing the framework for personal growth and ethical living.

The philosophical shift from divine-centric to self-centric beliefs

OVER THE COURSE OF history, human spirituality has undergone significant transformations, moving from a primarily divine-centric worldview to one that places greater emphasis on the self. In divine-centric beliefs, spirituality revolves around the existence and worship of gods or higher powers. These belief systems suggest that humans are dependent on divine beings for guidance, salvation, and understanding of life's purpose. The individual's spiritual journey is defined by their relationship with these external forces, and meaning is often found through faith, prayer, and adherence to religious doctrine.

However, as human thought evolved, so too did philosophical approaches to spirituality. The shift from divine-centric to self-centric beliefs marks a profound change in how individuals perceive their spiritual responsibilities and paths to fulfillment. In self-centric spiritual systems, the focus is no longer on external deities but on the individual's capacity for self-discovery, personal growth, and inner mastery. This transformation has been driven by a number of philosophical developments that emphasize the power and responsibility of the individual over divine intervention.

One of the earliest shifts can be seen in the rise of Eastern philosophies such as Buddhism and Jainism, where the focus moved away from deities and toward personal enlightenment. In these traditions, the self is seen as the key to liberation and spiritual awakening. For example, in Buddhism, the path to Nirvana is not through pleasing a god but through understanding the nature of the self and overcoming attachments, desires, and ignorance. Similarly, in Jainism, the purification of the soul is achieved through individual ethical action and discipline, not through divine favor.

The philosophical shift toward the self became more prominent in the West during the Enlightenment period, when reason and individualism began to challenge traditional religious authority. Philosophers like Immanuel Kant argued that morality and ethical living could be grounded in human reason rather than divine commands. This was a major turning point in the Western philosophical tradition, signaling a move toward human-centric ethics and away from the need for divine justification for moral decisions. Stoicism, too, offers an early example of self-centric spirituality, where the focus lies on personal virtue, emotional control, and rationality, teaching that one must master oneself to live a fulfilling life.

In modern times, the self-centric approach has further evolved into secular humanism and personal development movements. These philosophies suggest that individuals are fully capable of creating their own sense of purpose, morality, and fulfillment without relying on religious doctrine or a god. The rise of psychology and self-help movements in the 20th and 21st centuries has reinforced this shift, teaching that individuals hold the keys to their own well-being through introspection, self-discipline, and personal responsibility.

This philosophical transition reflects a broader change in how humans engage with spiritual questions and ethical challenges. As societies became more pluralistic and scientific knowledge expanded, the emphasis on divine authority in guiding human life diminished. People began to look inward for answers, recognizing that they had the capacity to shape their own destinies. This shift also aligns with the growing emphasis on autonomy and personal freedom in modern societies, where the individual's right to self-determination is highly valued.

In a self-centric spiritual framework, individuals are seen as their own spiritual authorities. They have the power to determine what is meaningful and right for themselves, and they are responsible for their own personal growth and ethical behavior. This shift from divine to self-centric beliefs has opened up new ways of understanding spirituality that are less dependent on external forces and more focused on cultivating inner peace, wisdom, and self-awareness.

Ultimately, the philosophical move from divine-centric to self-centric beliefs represents a major rethinking of what it means to live a spiritual life. Rather than seeking salvation or meaning through a god, individuals are now encouraged to explore their own potential, develop their own moral compass, and take responsibility for their spiritual journey. This transformation has made spirituality more personal, flexible, and deeply connected to the individual's experience, allowing for a more intimate and self-empowered approach to life's greatest questions.

Chapter 2: Buddhism – The Path to Enlightenment

Buddhism stands as one of the most profound spiritual traditions that focuses on the self as the central figure in the pursuit of enlightenment. Unlike many other religious systems, Buddhism does not rely on the existence of a creator god to explain the nature of the universe or the path to spiritual liberation. Instead, it places the individual at the heart of the journey toward truth, wisdom, and inner peace. The teachings of the Buddha, Siddhartha Gautama, offer a roadmap for personal transformation through self-realization and mindfulness, where one's thoughts, actions, and intentions become the foundation for spiritual growth.

Historically, Buddhism emerged as a response to the suffering and dissatisfaction that pervade human life. Rather than looking outward for divine intervention, the Buddha taught that the root of human suffering lies within the self—specifically in desires, attachments, and ignorance. By understanding and mastering these internal forces, individuals can achieve a state of Nirvana, a transcendent freedom from suffering, rebirth, and the cycle of existence known as samsara.

At the core of Buddhist practice is mindfulness, a disciplined awareness of one's thoughts, emotions, and actions. Through meditation and ethical living, practitioners work to cultivate this mindfulness, gradually peeling away the layers of illusion and self-deception that obscure their understanding of reality. In this sense, the path to enlightenment is deeply personal and internal, requiring sustained self-awareness and discipline.

This chapter explores the rich history of Buddhism and its core teachings, focusing on how self-realization and mindfulness serve as the pillars of the path to enlightenment. It also delves into the ultimate goal of Nirvana and how Buddhism offers a clear alternative to theistic religions, guiding individuals toward liberation through their own effort and insight, rather than reliance on a divine figure.

History and core teachings of Buddhism

BUDDHISM TRACES ITS origins to approximately 2,500 years ago in ancient India, founded by Siddhartha Gautama, who later became known as the Buddha, or the "Enlightened One." Siddhartha was born into a royal family in what is now modern-day Nepal. He lived a life of luxury and privilege, shielded from the hardships of the world. However, upon encountering the realities of old age, sickness, and death outside his palace, Siddhartha was struck by the suffering inherent in human existence. This realization prompted him to renounce his royal life in search of deeper truths about the nature of suffering and the path to liberation.

After years of intense meditation and spiritual exploration, Siddhartha attained enlightenment while meditating under the Bodhi tree. He realized the profound truth about the nature of human suffering and how to overcome it. His teachings, which formed the foundation of Buddhism, revolve around the Four Noble Truths and the Eightfold Path, which offer a practical guide to attaining enlightenment and escaping the cycle of rebirth, known as samsara.

The **Four Noble Truths** are the cornerstone of Buddhist philosophy. They are:

1. **The Truth of Suffering (Dukkha)**: All human life is marked by suffering, whether it be physical pain, emotional distress, or dissatisfaction. Even moments of joy are fleeting, making suffering an inevitable part of existence.

2. **The Truth of the Cause of Suffering (Samudaya)**: Suffering arises from attachment and desire. Humans cling to impermanent things—material possessions, relationships, and even life itself—which leads to inevitable pain when these things change or are lost.

3. **The Truth of the End of Suffering (Nirodha)**: Liberation from suffering is possible by extinguishing desire and attachment. This cessation of suffering leads to a state of Nirvana, where one is free from the cycle of birth and rebirth.

4. **The Truth of the Path to the End of Suffering (Magga)**: The path to ending suffering is through following the Eightfold Path, a set of ethical and mental practices that cultivate wisdom, ethical conduct, and mental discipline.

The **Eightfold Path** is a guide to living a life that leads to enlightenment. It consists of eight practices that are divided into three main categories: wisdom (prajna), ethical conduct (sila), and mental discipline (samadhi). The Eightfold Path is:

1. **Right Understanding**: Understanding the nature of reality, particularly the Four Noble Truths.

2. **Right Intention**: Cultivating the right attitudes and intentions, such as kindness and compassion, rather than selfish desires.

3. **Right Speech**: Speaking truthfully, kindly, and in a way that promotes harmony rather than harm.

4. **Right Action**: Engaging in ethical behavior that avoids harming others, including abstaining from killing, stealing, or engaging in sexual misconduct.

5. **Right Livelihood**: Pursuing a career or way of making a living that does not cause harm or suffering to others.

6. **Right Effort**: Cultivating positive states of mind and

avoiding unwholesome thoughts and emotions.

7. **Right Mindfulness**: Being fully aware and present in each moment, observing thoughts, emotions, and sensations without attachment or judgment.

8. **Right Concentration**: Practicing meditation to cultivate deep focus and mental tranquility, leading to the development of insight.

Buddhism teaches that the self is not a permanent, unchanging entity. Instead, it is composed of five aggregates (skandhas): form, sensation, perception, mental formations, and consciousness. These aggregates constantly change, which means there is no enduring self or soul as traditionally conceived in other spiritual traditions. This understanding of impermanence (anicca) and the non-self (anatta) is central to the Buddhist path to enlightenment. The goal of practice is to see through the illusion of a permanent self and overcome attachment to the transient aspects of existence.

Another key concept in Buddhism is **karma**, the law of moral cause and effect. Actions performed with intention—whether good or bad—generate karma, which influences the conditions of future rebirths. Positive actions lead to favorable outcomes, while negative actions lead to suffering. However, the ultimate aim is not just to accumulate good karma but to transcend the cycle of rebirth entirely by attaining Nirvana, a state of perfect peace and liberation from suffering.

As Buddhism spread beyond India, it evolved into different schools of thought, the most prominent being **Theravada** and **Mahayana** Buddhism. Theravada, often referred to as the "Teaching of the Elders," focuses on individual enlightenment and the monastic path. It emphasizes strict adherence to the original teachings of the Buddha and is prevalent in Southeast Asian countries like Thailand, Sri Lanka, and Myanmar. Mahayana Buddhism, which took root in East Asia, is more focused on the concept of the **Bodhisattva**, a being who attains enlightenment but remains in the world to help others achieve liberation. Mahayana places a strong emphasis on compassion and is practiced in countries such as China, Japan, and Korea.

Buddhism, therefore, offers a comprehensive framework for understanding suffering, its causes, and how to transcend it. At its core is the belief that through personal discipline, ethical behavior, and deep meditation, individuals can free themselves from the cycle of rebirth and suffering, attaining Nirvana, a state of eternal peace and liberation. The teachings of the Buddha provide a path of self-realization and mindfulness, showing that enlightenment is achieved not through divine intervention but through personal effort and insight.

The role of self-realization and mindfulness without a creator god

IN SPIRITUAL TRADITIONS that emphasize self-realization and mindfulness, the path to enlightenment or personal fulfillment is navigated without reliance on a creator god or external divine intervention. These traditions, such as Buddhism, Jainism, and modern secular mindfulness practices, teach that the individual holds the key to their own liberation or spiritual awakening. Unlike theistic religions, where salvation or enlightenment is often seen as a gift bestowed by a god, self-realization is a process of inward exploration and personal transformation.

The concept of **self-realization** revolves around understanding the true nature of the self and transcending the illusions and attachments that bind individuals to suffering. In these spiritual systems, the self is not considered a fixed or eternal soul but rather a dynamic entity shaped by thoughts, emotions, and experiences. The ultimate goal is to move beyond the ego's desires and attachments, which cloud true understanding, and to realize a state of pure awareness or enlightenment. This journey of self-realization is a personal one, requiring disciplined mental effort and ethical living, with the individual fully responsible for their own progress.

Mindfulness plays a crucial role in facilitating this process. Rooted in ancient practices but increasingly adopted in modern secular settings, mindfulness is the practice of maintaining a moment-to-moment awareness of thoughts, feelings, bodily sensations, and the surrounding environment. It is cultivated through techniques such as meditation, which focus on observing the mind without judgment, fostering a sense of inner peace and clarity. By being fully present and aware of one's mental and emotional states, individuals can better understand the causes of their suffering and take steps to alleviate it.

In traditions like Buddhism, mindfulness is one of the core elements of the path to enlightenment. The practice of **Right Mindfulness,** as outlined in the Eightfold Path, encourages individuals to become fully aware of their body, feelings, and mind in order to transcend attachments and delusions. Through sustained mindfulness, one learns to observe thoughts and emotions without becoming entangled in them, thereby gaining insight into the impermanent and interconnected nature of existence.

Without the need for a creator god, these systems place the responsibility for spiritual growth directly in the hands of the practitioner. The absence of a divine being does not imply a lack of spirituality or moral guidance; instead, it underscores the belief that true wisdom and peace arise from within. Individuals are encouraged to develop self-awareness, compassion, and wisdom through their own efforts, rather than relying on divine intervention or external validation.

Self-realization is closely tied to the concept of **liberation**—whether it's the Buddhist attainment of Nirvana or the Jain achievement of moksha (liberation from the cycle of rebirth).

These states represent the ultimate freedom from suffering and the end of the cycle of birth and death. They are reached not through prayer or divine grace but through the cultivation of mindfulness, ethical behavior, and self-discipline. By realizing the true nature of the self—free from ego and attachment—one can transcend suffering and reach a state of lasting peace.

In modern secular mindfulness practices, often detached from any religious framework, the emphasis is still on self-awareness and emotional regulation. Mindfulness-based stress reduction (MBSR) and other therapeutic applications of mindfulness demonstrate how these ancient practices can be used to enhance mental health and well-being, even without a spiritual or religious dimension. The focus remains on the self as the source of insight and healing, offering a path to emotional balance and clarity through personal awareness rather than divine intervention.

Thus, self-realization and mindfulness represent powerful tools for personal and spiritual growth in traditions that do not depend on the existence of a creator god. These practices affirm the ability of individuals to shape their own spiritual destiny, showing that enlightenment, liberation, and inner peace are accessible through dedicated effort and self-awareness. By looking inward and cultivating mindfulness, one can overcome the illusions and attachments that cause suffering, finding deeper meaning and fulfillment within themselves rather than seeking it from a higher power.

The pursuit of Nirvana

NIRVANA, ONE OF THE central concepts in Buddhism, represents the ultimate goal of spiritual practice: the complete liberation from suffering, desire, and the cycle of rebirth known as samsara. Unlike religious traditions that promise an afterlife in the presence of a god, Nirvana is not a place or state bestowed by a divine being; rather, it is a profound inner transformation that one achieves through self-realization and mental discipline. The pursuit of Nirvana is a deeply personal journey, requiring insight into the nature of existence and the mastery of one's own mind.

The word "Nirvana" literally means "blowing out" or "extinguishing," and it symbolizes the extinguishing of the fires of desire, hatred, and ignorance that fuel the cycle of suffering. In Buddhist teachings, these fires keep individuals bound to samsara, a cycle of birth, death, and rebirth that is marked by continuous suffering. This cycle is driven by attachment and craving—humans grasp for things that are impermanent, seeking pleasure and avoiding pain, which leads to dissatisfaction when those things inevitably change or disappear.

Achieving Nirvana requires a deep understanding of the Four Noble Truths, which outline the nature of suffering and the path to its cessation. The First Noble Truth teaches that suffering (dukkha) is an inherent part of life. The Second Noble Truth identifies the cause of suffering as attachment and desire (tanha). The Third Noble Truth holds that it is possible to end suffering by extinguishing desire, and the Fourth Noble Truth presents the Eightfold Path as the way to achieve this liberation.

The **Eightfold Path** provides a practical framework for living in a way that leads to Nirvana. It emphasizes ethical conduct, mental discipline, and wisdom. Key components of the path, such as Right Mindfulness and Right Concentration, involve training the mind to become fully aware of the present moment, free from distraction and attachment. By mastering mindfulness and meditation, practitioners develop the insight needed to see the true nature of reality, particularly the impermanence of all things (anicca) and the illusion of a permanent self (anatta).

One of the most significant challenges in the pursuit of Nirvana is overcoming the **illusion of the self**. In many spiritual traditions, the self is viewed as an eternal soul or essence, but Buddhism teaches that the self is a fluid and ever-changing collection of experiences, thoughts, and sensations. This concept, known as anatta or "no-self," is essential to Buddhist practice. The attachment to the idea of a permanent self leads to clinging, desire, and suffering. By realizing that the self is an illusion, individuals can let go of their attachments and desires, which is a key step on the path to Nirvana.

Nirvana is not a state of oblivion or non-existence, but rather a state of profound peace and freedom. It is characterized by the cessation of suffering, the end of all cravings, and a complete detachment from the ego and worldly desires. Those who attain Nirvana experience a deep sense of equanimity and compassion, as they are no longer driven by personal desires or aversions. They remain fully aware and engaged with the world, but without the emotional turmoil that arises from attachment and craving.

The path to Nirvana is a gradual one, requiring dedication and perseverance. It is often described as a path of purification—purifying the mind from the defilements of greed, hatred, and ignorance. This purification is achieved through the continuous practice of meditation, ethical conduct, and the cultivation of wisdom. Each step on the path brings deeper levels of insight and detachment, gradually freeing the practitioner from the mental habits that perpetuate suffering.

For many, Nirvana may seem like an unattainable ideal, but Buddhism teaches that every individual has the potential to reach this state through their own efforts. The Buddha himself is seen as a model of what is possible—he was not a divine being but a human who, through profound realization and practice, attained enlightenment and Nirvana. His teachings offer a blueprint for others to follow, showing that Nirvana is within reach for anyone willing to commit to the path of mindfulness, ethical living, and inner transformation.

In essence, the pursuit of Nirvana is the pursuit of ultimate freedom—freedom from the limitations of the ego, from the endless cycle of birth and death, and from the suffering that pervades human existence. It is a journey toward a state of pure awareness and peace, where the fires of desire and attachment have been extinguished, and the individual experiences a profound connection to the truth of existence. Nirvana, then, is not just an end to suffering but the realization of a deeper, timeless reality that lies beyond the transient world of samsara.

Chapter 3: Jainism – The Path of Non-Violence and Liberation

Jainism is a spiritual tradition that places immense importance on the purity and liberation of the soul through self-discipline, non-violence, and personal responsibility. At its core, Jainism teaches that the soul is inherently pure but becomes weighed down by karmic matter accumulated through attachment, desire, and harmful actions. Liberation, or *moksha*, is the ultimate goal, and it can only be achieved through the purification of the soul—something that each individual must accomplish through their own efforts.

One of the most defining principles of Jainism is *ahimsa*, or non-violence. This concept extends beyond physical harm to encompass thoughts, words, and deeds. In Jain philosophy, all living beings possess souls, and to harm another being is to accumulate negative karma that binds the soul to the cycle of birth and rebirth. By practicing non-violence in every aspect of life, individuals not only protect others but also purify their own soul, moving closer to liberation.

Jainism teaches that the self is the ultimate agent of its own liberation. There is no divine being who grants salvation or intervenes in the karmic process. Instead, personal responsibility, ethical behavior, and spiritual discipline are key. Through meditation, fasting, and strict adherence to non-violence, practitioners work toward freeing the soul from the bondage of karma and reaching a state of eternal bliss and freedom from the cycle of reincarnation.

This chapter delves into the teachings of Jainism, focusing on the soul's purification and the central role of *ahimsa* in self-mastery. It examines how Jainism, with its emphasis on personal effort and ethical living, offers a path to liberation that relies solely on the individual's actions and choices, making it a spiritual tradition that places the self at the forefront of the quest for freedom from suffering and rebirth.

Jain teachings on the soul and its purification

IN JAINISM, THE SOUL, or *jiva*, is seen as the fundamental essence of every living being. Unlike many other spiritual traditions that view the soul as pure or inherently good by default, Jainism teaches that the soul is often tainted by karma—an accumulation of moral impurities that bind the soul to the cycle of birth, death, and rebirth, known as samsara. The ultimate goal in Jainism is to purify the soul by removing the karma that has accumulated over countless lifetimes, leading to liberation or *moksha*.

Jain philosophy posits that the soul is eternal, independent, and full of knowledge, energy, and bliss in its pure state. However, as the soul interacts with the material world, it becomes encumbered by karmic particles that attach to it through actions, thoughts, and desires. These particles are not merely metaphysical concepts but are considered actual substances that weigh down the soul, obscuring its true nature. The more karmic particles one accumulates, the more distant the soul becomes from its pure, liberated state.

The process of accumulating karma in Jainism is heavily tied to the principle of non-violence, or *ahimsa*. Actions that cause harm to other living beings—whether physical harm, emotional harm, or even harm through careless thoughts—lead to the accumulation of negative karma. This is why *ahimsa* is such a central tenet of Jain practice. By living a life of strict non-violence, a Jain practitioner minimizes the karmic burden placed on the soul. The practice of non-violence extends beyond humans and animals to include all forms of life, down to the smallest organisms, reflecting the deep reverence Jains have for all living things.

Beyond *ahimsa*, there are other key practices aimed at purifying the soul. One of the most important is **self-discipline**, including practices such as fasting, meditation, and renunciation. Fasting helps to curb desires and attachments, which are seen as major sources of karmic accumulation. Meditation allows individuals to reflect on their actions, thoughts, and intentions, helping them to cultivate self-awareness and control over their impulses. Renunciation, which often includes a simple lifestyle and detachment from material possessions, further aids in reducing karmic attachment.

Jainism teaches that karma can be classified into two broad categories: **ghati karma** and **aghati karma**. Ghati karma is the type of karma that affects the qualities of the soul itself, such as knowledge, perception, and energy. This form of karma clouds the soul's inherent attributes, making it harder for individuals to understand the truth and achieve enlightenment. Aghati karma, on the other hand, impacts the physical body and external circumstances, such as health, lifespan, and social status. While both types of karma affect the soul's journey, ghati karma is considered more detrimental to spiritual progress, as it directly hinders the soul's purity and understanding.

Purification of the soul is achieved through the **three jewels** of Jainism: **right faith (samyak darshana), right knowledge (samyak jnana), and right conduct (samyak charitra)**. These three elements are interdependent and must be cultivated together for true spiritual progress. Right faith refers to a deep understanding and belief in the truths of Jain teachings, particularly the nature of the soul and karma. Right knowledge involves gaining a clear and accurate understanding of the nature of reality, free from ignorance and delusion. Right conduct encompasses ethical behavior and disciplined living, including adherence to non-violence, truthfulness, and chastity. Together, these three jewels form the foundation for the purification of the soul.

A key aspect of purifying the soul in Jainism is the concept of **karma shedding**, known as **nirjara**. Nirjara involves actively working to rid the soul of accumulated karma through penance, ascetic practices, and deep introspection. This is a gradual process, requiring a lifetime—or even many lifetimes—of dedication and effort. The practice of austerities, including fasting and various forms of self-restraint, is seen as a crucial part of this process. By enduring hardships willingly and refraining from harming others, individuals can accelerate the shedding of karma and move closer to liberation.

In Jain cosmology, the universe operates without a creator god, and liberation is a purely self-driven process. There is no divine being who grants salvation or intervenes in the karmic process. Instead, each soul must purify itself through its own actions and efforts. The ultimate state of liberation, or moksha, is when the soul is completely free from karma and rises to the top of the universe to dwell in a state of eternal bliss and omniscience, beyond the reach of suffering, death, and rebirth. In this liberated state, the soul exists in its true, pristine form—eternal, pure, and fully conscious.

For Jains, this journey of purifying the soul is both a moral and spiritual undertaking, requiring mindfulness of one's every thought, word, and action. It is a path of self-mastery, where the individual is fully responsible for their spiritual destiny. Through the disciplined practice of non-violence, ethical living, and self-restraint, the soul can gradually shed its karmic bonds and return to its natural state of purity and enlightenment. This pursuit of purification is at the heart of Jainism, guiding practitioners on their path to ultimate liberation.

Ahimsa (non-violence) and its role in self-mastery

AHIMSA, OR NON-VIOLENCE, is one of the most fundamental and revered principles in Jainism, as well as in other Indian spiritual traditions such as Buddhism and Hinduism. In Jain philosophy, ahimsa goes far beyond simply refraining from physical violence; it is a way of life that encompasses non-violence in thought, word, and deed. It is believed that every living being, no matter how small or seemingly insignificant, possesses a soul, and causing harm to any form of life accrues negative karma, which binds the soul to the cycle of samsara (birth, death, and rebirth). The practice of ahimsa, therefore, is essential for the purification of the soul and the ultimate attainment of moksha, or liberation.

In Jainism, the commitment to non-violence is absolute. It is not limited to avoiding physical harm to humans and animals, but extends to even the smallest forms of life, such as insects and microorganisms. This deep respect for all life stems from the belief that all living beings, regardless of size or level of consciousness, have the potential for spiritual growth and liberation. Every act of violence, no matter how small, is seen as a barrier to spiritual progress because it reinforces attachment and desire, both of which hinder the soul's journey toward purity.

Ahimsa is not just an ethical guideline; it is a form of **self-mastery**. Practicing non-violence requires constant mindfulness and discipline, as it encompasses every action, word, and thought. The practitioner must cultivate a heightened awareness of their interactions with the world, ensuring that they cause no harm—whether through direct action, negligence, or even harmful intentions. This requires a profound level of self-control, where the individual must actively manage their impulses, emotions, and desires in order to live in harmony with the principle of ahimsa.

The role of ahimsa in self-mastery is most evident in the way it shapes one's approach to life. A person committed to non-violence must exercise control over their anger, greed, and ego, as these emotions often lead to harmful actions. For example, anger might lead someone to harm another person, whether through harsh words or physical violence. Greed might lead to the exploitation of others or the environment. By practicing ahimsa, individuals learn to restrain these destructive impulses and instead cultivate qualities like compassion, patience, and humility. In doing so, they purify their own mind and soul, progressively freeing themselves from negative karma.

Additionally, ahimsa is directly connected to the practice of **detachment** in Jainism. Violence often arises from attachment—attachment to material possessions, status, relationships, or personal desires. When individuals are overly attached to these things, they are more likely to engage in harmful behaviors to protect or achieve what they desire. Practicing non-violence, therefore, also requires letting go of these attachments. By reducing one's attachment to the material world and to personal desires, an individual can cultivate a more peaceful and compassionate existence, free from the motivations that typically lead to violence.

The practice of ahimsa extends to one's **thoughts and intentions** as well. In Jainism, it is not enough to simply avoid physical harm to others; one must also cultivate non-violent thoughts and attitudes. Thoughts of hatred, jealousy, or ill-will are seen as forms of violence that damage the soul, even if they do not result in outward harm. Self-mastery through ahimsa, therefore, involves cultivating mental discipline and developing a mindset rooted in compassion and non-harm. Practitioners work to replace negative, harmful thoughts with positive, kind, and peaceful ones, thereby reducing the karmic burden on the soul.

Furthermore, **speech** is an important aspect of practicing ahimsa. Jainism teaches that words have the power to cause great harm, even when no physical violence is involved. Harsh, deceitful, or hurtful words can inflict emotional and psychological damage on others. Therefore, control over one's speech is crucial for living a life of non-violence. Practitioners are encouraged to speak truthfully, gently, and in a way that promotes peace and understanding, rather than conflict or harm. This discipline over speech is another vital aspect of self-mastery in the practice of ahimsa.

Ahimsa also plays a critical role in **ascetic practices** within Jainism. Many Jains, especially monks and nuns, go to great lengths to ensure they harm no living creature. For example, Jain ascetics may wear masks to avoid accidentally inhaling small insects, sweep the ground before walking to avoid stepping on tiny organisms, and follow a strict vegetarian or vegan diet to minimize harm to animals. These practices are not seen as extreme but as necessary steps in the purification of the soul and the fulfillment of the vow of non-violence. Such discipline demonstrates the deep commitment to self-mastery and the lengths to which practitioners go to minimize harm in every possible aspect of life.

In essence, ahimsa serves as both a moral and spiritual practice that guides Jains toward greater self-awareness, discipline, and control. It is a way to purify the soul by eliminating the causes of karmic bondage and promoting spiritual growth. Through non-violence, individuals not only protect other living beings but also nurture their own souls, advancing along the path to liberation. By mastering their thoughts, words, and actions, practitioners of ahimsa move closer to achieving a state of inner peace, purity, and ultimate freedom from the cycle of samsara.

In a world where violence—whether physical, verbal, or mental—is pervasive, the Jain commitment to ahimsa stands as a profound example of how self-mastery and non-violence can lead to both personal and spiritual transformation. Through the disciplined practice of non-harm, individuals not only contribute to a more peaceful world but also embark on a journey of self-purification, freeing themselves from the karmic consequences of violence and moving closer to the ultimate goal of moksha.

The self as the ultimate agent of liberation

IN JAINISM AND OTHER non-theistic spiritual traditions, the self is regarded as the ultimate force behind its own liberation. There is no divine being or external force responsible for delivering the soul from the cycle of samsara—birth, death, and rebirth. Instead, the individual must take full responsibility for their own spiritual journey. The path to liberation, or *moksha*, is deeply personal, requiring the soul to purify itself through self-discipline, ethical conduct, and the shedding of accumulated karma. This self-reliant approach emphasizes that each soul has the inherent potential to achieve liberation, but it must actively work toward that goal.

Jainism teaches that every living being possesses a soul (*jiva*) that is naturally pure, blissful, and full of knowledge. However, this pure state is obscured by karmic particles that attach to the soul through one's actions, thoughts, and desires. These particles weigh the soul down, trapping it in the cycle of samsara, and preventing it from experiencing its true nature. The journey toward liberation is, therefore, one of purification—removing the layers of karma that have accumulated over countless lifetimes. The individual is solely responsible for this process, as there is no divine grace or intervention that can purify the soul on their behalf.

In this framework, the self is not only the object of liberation but also the agent that initiates and sustains the process. The path to liberation requires a profound understanding of the self's role in generating karma, as well as the self-discipline needed to control one's thoughts, words, and actions. Jainism provides a detailed ethical system that guides individuals in this endeavor, emphasizing the importance of non-violence (*ahimsa*), truthfulness, non-stealing, chastity, and detachment from material possessions. These principles are not just moral guidelines; they are practical tools for reducing karmic accumulation and purifying the soul.

Self-mastery is a crucial component of the path to liberation. Since the soul itself is responsible for generating karma through attachment, desire, and ignorance, self-control becomes the key to breaking free from the cycle of suffering. Practitioners are encouraged to cultivate mindfulness and restraint in all aspects of life, including their thoughts, emotions, and physical actions. By developing mastery over their own impulses and desires, they can begin to dismantle the karmic bonds that tie them to the cycle of rebirth. This self-discipline is not seen as a form of punishment or asceticism for its own sake, but as a necessary practice for achieving spiritual freedom.

The concept of *nirjara*, or the shedding of karma, highlights the self's role as the agent of liberation. Nirjara involves the active effort to reduce and eventually eliminate karmic particles from the soul. This process can be accelerated through practices such as fasting, meditation, and the renunciation of worldly attachments. These ascetic practices help to weaken the hold of karma on the soul, allowing it to move closer to its natural, liberated state. Again, the responsibility for this process lies entirely with the individual—no external force can intervene in the process of nirjara. Liberation is attained solely through one's own actions and inner transformation.

This emphasis on the self as the agent of liberation is a radical departure from theistic religions, where divine beings often play a central role in granting salvation or enlightenment. In the Jain worldview, the universe operates on natural laws, and the soul's progress is governed by its own actions. There is no creator god to intervene in the process of karma or to absolve individuals of their past deeds. As a result, the individual must cultivate a deep sense of responsibility for their spiritual journey, understanding that every action, thought, and intention contributes to either their liberation or further entrapment in samsara.

In this self-driven approach to liberation, knowledge and awareness are key. Jain teachings emphasize the importance of *right faith, right knowledge*, and *right conduct*—the three jewels that guide individuals toward liberation. Right faith refers to a deep understanding of the nature of the soul, karma, and the path to moksha. Right knowledge involves acquiring accurate insights into reality, free from ignorance and delusion. Right conduct is the ethical discipline necessary to live in accordance with these truths, ensuring that one's actions align with the goal of liberation. Together, these three elements empower the individual to navigate the spiritual path with clarity and purpose, knowing that the self is both the seeker and the liberator.

Detachment plays a critical role in the self's journey toward liberation. Attachment to material possessions, relationships, or even one's own body can generate desire and suffering, further binding the soul to samsara. The practice of non-attachment, or *vairagya*, helps individuals to cultivate a sense of inner freedom, reducing their reliance on external sources of happiness. By recognizing the impermanence of the material world and the transient nature of desire, practitioners learn to focus on the purification of the soul, rather than the pursuit of fleeting pleasures. This detachment is not a rejection of life but a recognition that true freedom comes from within, not from external circumstances.

Ultimately, the self's role as the agent of liberation reinforces the idea that spiritual progress is a personal responsibility. Each individual must undertake the work of self-purification, mindfulness, and ethical living in order to free themselves from the cycle of suffering. The path to moksha is not a gift or reward given by a higher power—it is the natural outcome of a life lived with discipline, awareness, and a commitment to spiritual growth. By fully embracing the self as the source of both karma and liberation, Jainism offers a vision of spiritual freedom that is deeply empowering, placing the individual in control of their own destiny.

Chapter 4: Secular Humanism – Ethics Without a Deity

Secular humanism offers a vision of spirituality and ethical living that is rooted entirely in the human experience, without invoking the need for a god or divine authority. At its heart, secular humanism emphasizes the dignity, worth, and potential of every individual. It suggests that morality, meaning, and fulfillment can arise from human reason, empathy, and shared values, rather than from religious doctrines or divine commandments.

Humanism promotes a life guided by reason, critical thinking, and a commitment to ethical living based on the well-being of others. Rather than seeking moral guidance from sacred texts or spiritual intermediaries, humanists believe that humans are fully capable of making rational decisions about right and wrong. The focus is on improving human life—both individually and collectively—through compassion, fairness, and respect for human rights.

In a world where scientific knowledge and secular thought are increasingly shaping people's worldviews, secular humanism offers a pathway to spirituality that aligns with modern values. It champions the idea that ethical living can come from a commitment to reason and empathy, without the need for belief in a deity or an afterlife. Through this lens, life's purpose is derived from the pursuit of human flourishing, both at the personal level and for society as a whole.

This chapter explores the principles of secular humanism, focusing on how it provides an ethical framework for those who seek spirituality without theistic belief. By highlighting human dignity, rational thought, and ethical responsibility, secular humanism presents a compelling alternative for individuals who desire a fulfilling spiritual life grounded in human experience, community, and shared values, without relying on divine guidance.

Overview of humanism and secular spirituality

HUMANISM, PARTICULARLY in its modern form, is a philosophy that emphasizes human values, reason, and ethical responsibility without reliance on the supernatural or divine intervention. Rooted in the belief that human beings have the ability to lead meaningful and moral lives based on reason and empathy, humanism rejects the need for religious frameworks to guide ethical decisions or provide meaning. Instead, it posits that people can cultivate a fulfilling existence by focusing on the well-being of humanity, the pursuit of knowledge, and the development of personal and communal virtues.

Secular spirituality is closely aligned with humanism but extends the concept by incorporating practices and experiences that are often associated with traditional spirituality, such as mindfulness, meditation, a deep sense of connection to the universe, and an appreciation for the awe-inspiring aspects of life. What differentiates secular spirituality from religious spirituality is the absence of a belief in a higher power or the divine. Instead, secular spirituality emphasizes the sacredness of life itself and the interconnectedness of all beings, grounding the spiritual experience in the natural world and in human relationships.

At the heart of humanism is the idea that humans, through their capacity for reason, compassion, and critical thinking, can create ethical systems that promote the common good. Humanists believe that morality does not come from divine commandments but from human experience and empathy. The ability to discern right from wrong is seen as an innate quality that can be cultivated and refined through education, dialogue, and self-reflection. Humanism emphasizes responsibility to others, promoting ideas such as human rights, equality, social justice, and environmental stewardship, all of which are framed within a secular worldview.

This secular worldview does not dismiss the importance of spirituality, but it redefines it in non-theistic terms. Secular spirituality recognizes that humans seek a deeper connection to something larger than themselves, whether that be the universe, the natural world, or the human community. It focuses on personal growth, self-awareness, and emotional well-being as central to the spiritual experience. Practices like mindfulness, meditation, and even artistic expression are embraced as ways to explore one's inner life, achieve mental clarity, and cultivate a sense of peace and purpose. These practices help individuals develop a more profound understanding of themselves and their place in the world, without needing to invoke the supernatural.

In secular spirituality, the concept of transcendence is redefined. Rather than being understood as communion with a higher power, transcendence in this context refers to experiences that help individuals rise above ordinary, everyday concerns and gain a broader perspective on life. This might occur through deep contemplation, a connection with nature, or acts of kindness and service to others. These experiences foster a sense of meaning and fulfillment, grounded in the understanding that life is precious and finite. There is often a focus on the present moment, with mindfulness and an appreciation for the "here and now" being key elements of secular spirituality.

Humanism, with its focus on reason and ethics, complements secular spirituality by providing a framework for how to live a good life without the need for religious belief. Together, they offer an approach to life that is rational, compassionate, and spiritually fulfilling. Humanism encourages the use of science, critical thinking, and dialogue to understand the world, while secular spirituality adds a personal dimension, encouraging individuals to explore their inner lives, emotional health, and sense of purpose.

This approach to spirituality and ethics appeals to those who may feel disconnected from traditional religious structures or who seek a more personal, self-directed path to meaning. It provides a flexible framework that allows for spiritual growth without requiring adherence to dogma. Many who embrace humanism and secular spirituality find that it aligns well with their values of autonomy, personal responsibility, and a commitment to improving the world through human action.

At the same time, secular spirituality offers a space for those who appreciate the ritual, reflection, and community aspects of spirituality without the theistic elements. Practices such as group meditation, nature retreats, or philosophical discussions can serve as secular counterparts to religious gatherings, providing opportunities for connection, reflection, and shared values. These experiences foster a sense of belonging and support, while encouraging individuals to think critically about their lives and the world around them.

In essence, humanism and secular spirituality provide a path for those who seek meaning, purpose, and ethical living without relying on religious frameworks. They emphasize the importance of human agency, the cultivation of inner peace, and the responsibility to contribute positively to the world. By encouraging individuals to find fulfillment through self-awareness, compassion, and an appreciation for life's beauty, these philosophies offer a rich and profound alternative to traditional spiritual beliefs. Through this lens, spirituality becomes an exploration of what it means to be human—our relationships with ourselves, each other, and the world we inhabit—without the need for divine guidance or religious doctrine.

The emphasis on human dignity, reason, and ethics in guiding spiritual life

HUMANISM PLACES THE utmost importance on the inherent dignity of every individual. This principle is foundational to its worldview, asserting that all people deserve respect, freedom, and the opportunity to live fulfilling lives, regardless of their religious beliefs, background, or social status. Human dignity, in this context, is not derived from divine authority or supernatural edicts, but from the recognition of shared humanity and the capacity for reason and ethical living. The emphasis on human dignity leads to a moral philosophy centered around compassion, justice, and the protection of individual rights, which guides the way humanists approach life and the world.

Reason, as a guiding force, is critical in humanist and secular philosophies. Humanism rejects the need for supernatural explanations, instead advocating for the use of logic, scientific inquiry, and critical thinking as tools to understand the world and navigate life's challenges. This reliance on reason does not diminish the complexity or beauty of life but enhances it by encouraging individuals to explore and appreciate the natural world and human experience with clarity and insight. Through reason, humanists believe that humanity can progress—solving social issues, improving lives, and creating a more equitable world.

In the realm of ethics, reason plays a vital role in determining what is just and moral. Unlike religious systems where moral laws are often decreed by a god or contained in sacred texts, humanism asserts that ethical principles arise from human nature and shared experiences. Moral values such as kindness, fairness, and the respect for others emerge from our capacity for empathy and our understanding of the consequences of our actions. Ethics, then, is not a set of rigid commandments, but a dynamic process of reflection, dialogue, and understanding, always centered on the idea of promoting human dignity and well-being.

This focus on human dignity and reason leads to an ethical system grounded in principles such as equality, compassion, and mutual respect. Humanists argue that every person has the right to pursue happiness, freedom, and self-actualization, as long as it does not infringe on the rights of others. This notion of mutual respect informs the humanist commitment to social justice, human rights, and democratic governance. Societal structures, under this framework, are built to protect the dignity and rights of individuals, promoting the idea that a fair and just society is one where all people can thrive.

The commitment to **ethics** in humanism is not a passive or abstract ideal but a practical guide for everyday life. Humanists believe that individuals have a responsibility to act ethically, not because of divine commandment or fear of punishment, but because it is the right thing to do. This moral imperative arises from an understanding of the interconnectedness of all people and the recognition that our actions have real, tangible impacts on the lives of others. Therefore, personal choices, from the way one treats others to how one contributes to the community, are seen as essential aspects of living a good and meaningful life.

In guiding spiritual life, the focus on reason and ethics does not exclude the possibility of emotional depth or spiritual experiences. Humanists and secular spiritualists often find profound meaning in relationships, personal growth, art, nature, and the pursuit of knowledge. The spiritual dimension of humanism is grounded in the awe and wonder of existence—the beauty of the natural world, the mystery of consciousness, and the complexity of human experience. Spirituality, for humanists, is about living authentically, cultivating empathy, and engaging with the world in a thoughtful and ethical way, not through religious rituals or worship, but through deliberate, mindful living.

Human dignity is central to this way of life. The recognition that each person is valuable in their own right leads to a sense of responsibility to others. This emphasis on the shared humanity of all people motivates actions rooted in compassion, whether it be working to alleviate suffering, fighting for social equality, or simply treating others with kindness in daily interactions. Respecting the dignity of others is not just a social obligation; it is a spiritual practice that affirms the interconnectedness of all human beings.

In practice, this means creating and nurturing a community where fairness, empathy, and inclusion are prioritized. Ethical decision-making becomes about striving for the greater good and recognizing that human life is finite and precious, making each moment an opportunity to create positive change. This approach to spirituality is centered on action—choosing to live a life that reflects one's values and using reason and compassion to navigate moral complexities.

In a world often fraught with division, misunderstanding, and inequality, humanism's emphasis on dignity, reason, and ethics provides a framework for building bridges rather than walls. It offers a way to engage with life's challenges in a thoughtful and constructive manner, recognizing that while humans may not have all the answers, they have the capacity to learn, grow, and improve both individually and collectively.

Ultimately, the emphasis on human dignity, reason, and ethics in humanism and secular spirituality offers a path to living with integrity and purpose. It shifts the focus from external authorities and divine expectations to the intrinsic value of each person and the collective responsibility to create a world where everyone can flourish. This approach to spiritual life is grounded in the belief that through reason, empathy, and ethical action, individuals can lead meaningful lives, contributing to the betterment of themselves and society, without the need for divine guidance.

Veganism as a lifestyle rooted in non-violence,

compassion, and self-discipline

VEGANISM IS MORE THAN just a dietary choice; it is a lifestyle that is deeply rooted in the principles of non-violence, compassion, and self-discipline. At its core, veganism is driven by the desire to cause the least amount of harm to living beings and the environment. This commitment extends far beyond what one eats—it encompasses all aspects of life, including clothing, products, and the general impact one has on the world. For many, veganism is a conscious effort to live in alignment with ethical beliefs, ensuring that daily actions reflect a deep respect for the well-being of all sentient creatures.

The principle of **non-violence**, or *ahimsa*, is central to the vegan philosophy. Ahimsa, originating from spiritual traditions such as Jainism, Buddhism, and Hinduism, promotes a life of non-harm to other living beings. In the context of veganism, this means avoiding the consumption or use of animal products, as the production of meat, dairy, eggs, and other animal-derived items often involves the exploitation, suffering, and killing of animals. Vegans believe that since animals are capable of feeling pain and suffering, causing harm to them for food, clothing, or any other purpose is morally wrong. This belief drives the decision to abstain from all forms of animal exploitation, choosing instead to support practices that minimize suffering and protect animal rights.

In addition to the commitment to non-violence, **compassion** plays a significant role in the vegan lifestyle. Compassion involves not only empathy for the suffering of others but also the willingness to take action to alleviate that suffering. Veganism is an expression of this compassion, as it is based on the belief that animals should not be subjected to cruelty or suffering for human consumption or convenience. Many vegans are motivated by the recognition that animals, like humans, have the capacity to experience joy, fear, and pain, and they believe it is unjust to inflict suffering upon them for the sake of human desires. By choosing a vegan lifestyle, individuals align their actions with their compassionate values, working to create a more just and ethical world for all living beings.

This sense of compassion also extends to the environment. Veganism is often seen as a way to reduce one's ecological footprint, as the production of animal products requires significantly more resources—such as water, land, and energy—than plant-based alternatives. Additionally, the animal agriculture industry is a major contributor to deforestation, habitat destruction, and greenhouse gas emissions, all of which have devastating effects on ecosystems and contribute to climate change. For many vegans, the choice to abstain from animal products is not only about compassion for animals but also about protecting the planet and ensuring a sustainable future for all species.

Self-discipline is another crucial component of veganism, as maintaining a vegan lifestyle requires mindful decision-making and a strong sense of personal responsibility. Choosing to avoid animal products, particularly in a world where they are pervasive, demands a heightened awareness of one's habits, surroundings, and options. Whether it's selecting plant-based alternatives, researching cruelty-free products, or adjusting social behaviors, vegans must constantly practice self-control to align their daily choices with their ethical convictions. This discipline is not about deprivation but about living intentionally and ensuring that one's actions are in harmony with personal values.

For many vegans, this practice of self-discipline extends beyond dietary choices to encompass all areas of life, including the consumption of clothing, cosmetics, and other goods. The commitment to avoid products that involve animal testing, animal ingredients, or environmentally destructive practices requires an ongoing dedication to ethical living. It involves researching brands, reading labels, and making informed decisions, all of which reflect a deep commitment to personal integrity and the principles of non-violence and compassion.

The practice of veganism also requires resilience, especially in social settings where the majority of people may not share the same values. Vegans often face challenges such as limited food options, social pressure, or criticism for their lifestyle choices. In these situations, self-discipline becomes essential for maintaining the commitment to vegan principles, as it empowers individuals to stay true to their beliefs even in the face of external challenges. This resilience is part of the larger ethical and spiritual journey of veganism, where individuals continually strive to live in accordance with their deepest values, despite the obstacles that may arise.

Veganism, therefore, is not just a dietary or consumer choice—it is a lifestyle that fosters a sense of connection and responsibility to all living beings. By adhering to principles of non-violence, compassion, and self-discipline, vegans aim to reduce harm and promote a more ethical and sustainable world. It is a lifestyle that challenges individuals to consider the far-reaching impacts of their actions and to cultivate a deeper awareness of their role in the interconnected web of life.

Ultimately, veganism encourages a more mindful and intentional way of living. It pushes individuals to reflect on the ethical implications of their choices and to actively seek ways to live with greater compassion and integrity. In a world where animals, the environment, and even human health are often sacrificed for convenience and profit, veganism offers an alternative that prioritizes non-harm and respect for life. Through the practice of veganism, individuals can engage in a daily act of compassion, contribute to the well-being of the planet, and align their lives with values of kindness, empathy, and justice.

How being vegan is part of a broader spiritual journey for many

FOR MANY INDIVIDUALS, veganism is not just a lifestyle choice or a dietary decision—it is an integral part of a broader spiritual journey that emphasizes connection, compassion, and living in alignment with one's deepest values. In this sense, veganism transcends the act of abstaining from animal products and becomes a pathway toward personal growth, ethical living, and spiritual awareness. By embracing veganism, many people find themselves engaging in a profound exploration of their beliefs about the world, their relationship with other living beings, and their role in the larger ecosystem of life.

At the heart of this spiritual journey is the concept of **compassion**—a central tenet in many spiritual traditions. Whether rooted in Eastern philosophies such as Buddhism and Jainism, which emphasize non-harm (*ahimsa*), or in modern secular humanism, compassion is often viewed as the foundation of an ethical and spiritual life. For vegans, the decision to avoid animal products is a direct expression of this compassion, as it reflects a conscious choice to minimize harm and suffering. By refusing to participate in industries that exploit or harm animals, vegans align their actions with a sense of moral responsibility toward other sentient beings, recognizing their capacity for pain, fear, and joy.

This sense of compassion also extends beyond animals to encompass a broader awareness of the interconnectedness of all life. Many who embrace veganism do so as part of a desire to live in harmony with the planet, recognizing that the exploitation of animals is linked to environmental degradation, climate change, and the depletion of natural resources. For these individuals, veganism becomes a way to practice **environmental stewardship**, which is often seen as a spiritual duty. By reducing their environmental footprint through plant-based living, they honor the Earth and seek to preserve it for future generations. In this way, veganism is part of a holistic spiritual practice that includes care for the environment and a commitment to sustainability.

Mindfulness also plays a crucial role in the spiritual dimension of veganism. The choice to live vegan requires a heightened awareness of one's daily habits and consumption patterns. It involves being mindful of not just what one eats, but also the broader impact of one's actions on the world—whether it's in the products one purchases, the businesses one supports, or the lifestyle choices one makes. This mindfulness encourages individuals to be more intentional in their decisions, fostering a deeper sense of personal responsibility and a stronger connection to their values. Many vegans find that this practice of mindfulness extends beyond their dietary choices, leading them to explore other areas of their life where they can live more consciously and ethically.

For those on a spiritual path, veganism is often seen as a form of **self-discipline** and **purification**. Just as many spiritual traditions encourage fasting or renunciation of material desires as a means of cultivating inner clarity, veganism can be viewed as a practice of renouncing the consumption of animal products in favor of a more compassionate and ethical way of living. This self-discipline helps individuals cultivate a sense of control over their desires and urges, which in turn supports their spiritual growth. By practicing restraint and making conscious choices that align with their values, vegans feel a deeper sense of spiritual fulfillment, knowing they are contributing to the well-being of the world and living in a way that reflects their ethical beliefs.

For some, veganism is also a step toward greater **spiritual alignment**. Many who adopt a vegan lifestyle report feeling more at peace with themselves, knowing that their actions are consistent with their spiritual or ethical ideals. This alignment between beliefs and actions is an essential aspect of many spiritual journeys, as it fosters a sense of integrity and authenticity. By living in a way that actively reduces harm and promotes kindness, individuals feel that they are living in accordance with their spiritual convictions, which strengthens their sense of purpose and connection to something greater than themselves.

Additionally, the sense of **interconnectedness** that veganism fosters is a significant aspect of the broader spiritual journey for many. Veganism encourages individuals to recognize their place within the web of life, emphasizing the idea that all living beings are interconnected and that our actions have ripple effects throughout the ecosystem. This understanding leads to a deeper sense of responsibility toward both animals and the planet, as well as a recognition of the profound impact that one's choices can have on the world. For many, this awareness fosters a deep sense of spiritual connection to all life, helping them to feel more attuned to the natural world and to the ethical implications of their actions.

Veganism can also lead to spiritual growth by encouraging **compassionate action**. Many spiritual traditions emphasize the importance of service to others, and veganism is often seen as a form of service—not only to animals but also to the environment and future generations. By adopting a lifestyle that seeks to reduce harm and promote well-being, vegans engage in a form of active compassion, contributing to a world that is more just, equitable, and sustainable. This sense of compassionate action reinforces their spiritual path, as it provides a tangible way to live out their values and contribute to the greater good.

For many, the journey of veganism becomes intertwined with their larger spiritual quest for peace, harmony, and enlightenment. As they deepen their understanding of non-harm, mindfulness, and ethical living, they find that veganism offers a powerful way to cultivate spiritual awareness in their everyday lives. It challenges them to live with greater intention, to be more compassionate, and to see their choices as part of a larger moral and spiritual framework.

Ultimately, for those who view veganism as part of their broader spiritual journey, it is not just about abstaining from certain foods or products—it is about living in alignment with their deepest values. It is about practicing compassion, mindfulness, and ethical responsibility in all aspects of life. Veganism becomes a spiritual practice in itself, one that reflects a commitment to creating a more compassionate, just, and harmonious world for all living beings. Through this practice, individuals on a spiritual path find greater peace, purpose, and fulfillment, knowing that their actions contribute to the well-being of others and to the greater whole.

Chapter 5: Veganism – Ethics, Self-Control, and Spiritual Discipline

Veganism, often seen as a dietary choice, extends far beyond what one eats—it is a lifestyle rooted in the principles of non-violence, compassion, and self-discipline. For many, the choice to live a vegan life is part of a broader spiritual journey that seeks to align their actions with their ethical and moral beliefs. At its core, veganism is about reducing harm to other living beings and fostering a deep respect for all forms of life, making it not just a dietary decision, but a spiritual and ethical practice.

The principle of non-violence, or *ahimsa*, is central to veganism. By choosing not to consume or use products derived from animals, vegans commit to a life of compassion, where minimizing harm to animals and the environment becomes a moral imperative. This commitment reflects a spiritual discipline that values the interconnectedness of life and recognizes that personal choices have profound ethical implications.

For many, the practice of veganism is not just about what they refrain from consuming but about cultivating self-control, mindfulness, and intentional living. By making conscious choices in everyday life, individuals on a vegan path practice self-discipline, which strengthens their spiritual well-being. These choices can create a sense of harmony between their values and their actions, fostering inner peace and a deeper connection to the world around them.

This chapter delves into how veganism serves as a spiritual practice for many, focusing on its ethical foundations and the discipline it requires. It explores how adopting a vegan lifestyle connects personal choices to spiritual growth, encouraging individuals to live in a way that honors both their own well-being and the well-being of other living beings. By aligning one's actions with values of compassion and non-violence, veganism becomes more than just a lifestyle—it becomes a spiritual path rooted in ethical living.

Veganism as a lifestyle rooted in non-violence, compassion, and self-discipline

VEGANISM IS MORE THAN just a dietary choice; it is a lifestyle that is deeply rooted in the principles of non-violence, compassion, and self-discipline. At its core, veganism is driven by the desire to cause the least amount of harm to living beings and the environment. This commitment extends far beyond what one eats—it encompasses all aspects of life, including clothing, products, and the general impact one has on the world. For many, veganism is a conscious effort to live in alignment with ethical beliefs, ensuring that daily actions reflect a deep respect for the well-being of all sentient creatures.

The principle of **non-violence**, or *ahimsa*, is central to the vegan philosophy. Ahimsa, originating from spiritual traditions such as Jainism, Buddhism, and Hinduism, promotes a life of non-harm to other living beings. In the context of veganism, this means avoiding the consumption or use of animal products, as the production of meat, dairy, eggs, and other animal-derived items often involves the exploitation, suffering, and killing of animals. Vegans believe that since animals are capable of feeling pain and suffering, causing harm to them for food, clothing, or any other purpose is morally wrong. This belief drives the decision to abstain from all forms of animal exploitation, choosing instead to support practices that minimize suffering and protect animal rights.

In addition to the commitment to non-violence, **compassion** plays a significant role in the vegan lifestyle. Compassion involves not only empathy for the suffering of others but also the willingness to take action to alleviate that suffering. Veganism is an expression of this compassion, as it is based on the belief that animals should not be subjected to cruelty or suffering for human consumption or convenience. Many vegans are motivated by the recognition that animals, like humans, have the capacity to experience joy, fear, and pain, and they believe it is unjust to inflict suffering upon them for the sake of human desires. By choosing a vegan lifestyle, individuals align their actions with their compassionate values, working to create a more just and ethical world for all living beings.

This sense of compassion also extends to the environment. Veganism is often seen as a way to reduce one's ecological footprint, as the production of animal products requires significantly more resources—such as water, land, and energy—than plant-based alternatives. Additionally, the animal agriculture industry is a major contributor to deforestation, habitat destruction, and greenhouse gas emissions, all of which have devastating effects on ecosystems and contribute to climate change. For many vegans, the choice to abstain from animal products is not only about compassion for animals but also about protecting the planet and ensuring a sustainable future for all species.

Self-discipline is another crucial component of veganism, as maintaining a vegan lifestyle requires mindful decision-making and a strong sense of personal responsibility. Choosing to avoid animal products, particularly in a world where they are pervasive, demands a heightened awareness of one's habits, surroundings, and options. Whether it's selecting plant-based alternatives, researching cruelty-free products, or adjusting social behaviors, vegans must constantly practice self-control to align their daily choices with their ethical convictions.

This discipline is not about deprivation but about living intentionally and ensuring that one's actions are in harmony with personal values.

For many vegans, this practice of self-discipline extends beyond dietary choices to encompass all areas of life, including the consumption of clothing, cosmetics, and other goods. The commitment to avoid products that involve animal testing, animal ingredients, or environmentally destructive practices requires an ongoing dedication to ethical living. It involves researching brands, reading labels, and making informed decisions, all of which reflect a deep commitment to personal integrity and the principles of non-violence and compassion.

The practice of veganism also requires resilience, especially in social settings where the majority of people may not share the same values. Vegans often face challenges such as limited food options, social pressure, or criticism for their lifestyle choices. In these situations, self-discipline becomes essential for maintaining the commitment to vegan principles, as it empowers individuals to stay true to their beliefs even in the face of external challenges. This resilience is part of the larger ethical and spiritual journey of veganism, where individuals continually strive to live in accordance with their deepest values, despite the obstacles that may arise.

Veganism, therefore, is not just a dietary or consumer choice—it is a lifestyle that fosters a sense of connection and responsibility to all living beings. By adhering to principles of non-violence, compassion, and self-discipline, vegans aim to reduce harm and promote a more ethical and sustainable world. It is a lifestyle that challenges individuals to consider the far-reaching impacts of their actions and to cultivate a deeper awareness of their role in the interconnected web of life.

Ultimately, veganism encourages a more mindful and intentional way of living. It pushes individuals to reflect on the ethical implications of their choices and to actively seek ways to live with greater compassion and integrity. In a world where animals, the environment, and even human health are often sacrificed for convenience and profit, veganism offers an alternative that prioritizes non-harm and respect for life. Through the practice of veganism, individuals can engage in a daily act of compassion, contribute to the well-being of the planet, and align their lives with values of kindness, empathy, and justice.

How being vegan is part of a broader spiritual journey for many

FOR MANY INDIVIDUALS, veganism is not just a lifestyle choice or a dietary decision—it is an integral part of a broader spiritual journey that emphasizes connection, compassion, and living in alignment with one's deepest values. In this sense, veganism transcends the act of abstaining from animal products and becomes a pathway toward personal growth, ethical living, and spiritual awareness. By embracing veganism, many people find themselves engaging in a profound exploration of their beliefs about the world, their relationship with other living beings, and their role in the larger ecosystem of life.

At the heart of this spiritual journey is the concept of **compassion**—a central tenet in many spiritual traditions. Whether rooted in Eastern philosophies such as Buddhism and Jainism, which emphasize non-harm (*ahimsa*), or in modern secular humanism, compassion is often viewed as the foundation of an ethical and spiritual life. For vegans, the decision to avoid animal products is a direct expression of this compassion, as it reflects a conscious choice to minimize harm and suffering. By refusing to participate in industries that exploit or harm animals, vegans align their actions with a sense of moral responsibility toward other sentient beings, recognizing their capacity for pain, fear, and joy.

This sense of compassion also extends beyond animals to encompass a broader awareness of the interconnectedness of all life.

Many who embrace veganism do so as part of a desire to live in harmony with the planet, recognizing that the exploitation of animals is linked to environmental degradation, climate change, and the depletion of natural resources. For these individuals, veganism becomes a way to practice **environmental stewardship**, which is often seen as a spiritual duty. By reducing their environmental footprint through plant-based living, they honor the Earth and seek to preserve it for future generations. In this way, veganism is part of a holistic spiritual practice that includes care for the environment and a commitment to sustainability.

Mindfulness also plays a crucial role in the spiritual dimension of veganism. The choice to live vegan requires a heightened awareness of one's daily habits and consumption patterns. It involves being mindful of not just what one eats, but also the broader impact of one's actions on the world—whether it's in the products one purchases, the businesses one supports, or the lifestyle choices one makes. This mindfulness encourages individuals to be more intentional in their decisions, fostering a deeper sense of personal responsibility and a stronger connection to their values. Many vegans find that this practice of mindfulness extends beyond their dietary choices, leading them to explore other areas of their life where they can live more consciously and ethically.

For those on a spiritual path, veganism is often seen as a form of **self-discipline** and **purification**. Just as many spiritual traditions encourage fasting or renunciation of material desires as a means of cultivating inner clarity, veganism can be viewed as a practice of renouncing the consumption of animal products in favor of a more compassionate and ethical way of living. This self-discipline helps individuals cultivate a sense of control over their desires and urges, which in turn supports their spiritual growth. By practicing restraint and making conscious choices that align with their values, vegans feel a deeper sense of spiritual fulfillment, knowing they are contributing to the well-being of the world and living in a way that reflects their ethical beliefs.

For some, veganism is also a step toward greater **spiritual alignment**. Many who adopt a vegan lifestyle report feeling more at peace with themselves, knowing that their actions are consistent with their spiritual or ethical ideals. This alignment between beliefs and actions is an essential aspect of many spiritual journeys, as it fosters a sense of integrity and authenticity. By living in a way that actively reduces harm and promotes kindness, individuals feel that they are living in accordance with their spiritual convictions, which strengthens their sense of purpose and connection to something greater than themselves.

Additionally, the sense of **interconnectedness** that veganism fosters is a significant aspect of the broader spiritual journey for many. Veganism encourages individuals to recognize their place within the web of life, emphasizing the idea that all living beings are interconnected and that our actions have ripple effects throughout the ecosystem. This understanding leads to a deeper sense of responsibility toward both animals and the planet, as well as a recognition of the profound impact that one's choices can have on the world. For many, this awareness fosters a deep sense of spiritual connection to all life, helping them to feel more attuned to the natural world and to the ethical implications of their actions.

Veganism can also lead to spiritual growth by encouraging **compassionate action**. Many spiritual traditions emphasize the importance of service to others, and veganism is often seen as a form of service—not only to animals but also to the environment and future generations. By adopting a lifestyle that seeks to reduce harm and promote well-being, vegans engage in a form of active compassion, contributing to a world that is more just, equitable, and sustainable. This sense of compassionate action reinforces their spiritual path, as it provides a tangible way to live out their values and contribute to the greater good.

For many, the journey of veganism becomes intertwined with their larger spiritual quest for peace, harmony, and enlightenment. As they deepen their understanding of non-harm, mindfulness, and ethical living, they find that veganism offers a powerful way to cultivate spiritual awareness in their everyday lives. It challenges them to live with greater intention, to be more compassionate, and to see their choices as part of a larger moral and spiritual framework.

Ultimately, for those who view veganism as part of their broader spiritual journey, it is not just about abstaining from certain foods or products—it is about living in alignment with their deepest values. It is about practicing compassion, mindfulness, and ethical responsibility in all aspects of life. Veganism becomes a spiritual practice in itself, one that reflects a commitment to creating a more compassionate, just, and harmonious world for all living beings. Through this practice, individuals on a spiritual path find greater peace, purpose, and fulfillment, knowing that their actions contribute to the well-being of others and to the greater whole.

Connections between personal choices and spiritual well-being

THE CHOICES INDIVIDUALS make in their daily lives are deeply intertwined with their sense of spiritual well-being. Every action, whether seemingly small or significant, reflects personal values, beliefs, and the degree to which one aligns their behavior with their ethical or spiritual ideals. For many, personal choices are not just practical decisions—they are expressions of their spiritual path, serving as a means of cultivating inner peace, moral integrity, and a deeper connection to the world around them. These choices shape not only the outer reality of a person's life but also their inner sense of harmony, purpose, and fulfillment.

One of the most profound ways in which personal choices influence spiritual well-being is through the concept of **integrity**. When individuals make decisions that are consistent with their values—whether those values are rooted in compassion, non-violence, mindfulness, or justice—they experience a sense of wholeness and alignment. This integrity, or congruence between belief and action, strengthens one's spiritual foundation. When actions reflect deeply held convictions, individuals feel more authentic and grounded, leading to a greater sense of peace and satisfaction. Conversely, when personal choices conflict with one's values, it can create inner tension, guilt, or dissonance, undermining one's spiritual equilibrium.

For example, many people who follow spiritual paths centered on compassion, such as veganism or environmentalism, see their daily choices as a direct extension of their spiritual beliefs. The decision to eat plant-based foods, reduce consumption of animal products, or support sustainable practices are not merely practical considerations but acts of living in alignment with the principle of non-harm (*ahimsa*). These choices reinforce a sense of moral clarity and contribute to spiritual well-being because they reflect an ongoing commitment to reducing suffering and caring for the Earth. This alignment between actions and ethics deepens a person's connection to their spiritual path and fosters a sense of purpose that transcends individual needs.

Mindfulness, another important aspect of many spiritual traditions, encourages individuals to be fully present in the moment and to make conscious, deliberate choices. This practice of mindful decision-making enhances spiritual well-being by fostering greater awareness of the impact of one's actions, both on oneself and on others. When individuals are mindful, they are more likely to make choices that reflect their true values, rather than acting out of habit, convenience, or societal pressure. Whether it's choosing how to respond in a difficult situation, selecting the foods they eat, or deciding how to spend their time, mindfulness encourages intentionality and reduces the likelihood of acting in ways that are contrary to one's spiritual goals.

The relationship between personal choices and spiritual well-being is also closely linked to the concept of **self-discipline**. Many spiritual traditions emphasize the importance of self-restraint and conscious effort in achieving personal growth and enlightenment. Self-discipline enables individuals to align their actions with their higher spiritual aims, whether that involves cultivating compassion, overcoming destructive habits, or practicing ethical living. Every choice becomes a reflection of the level of discipline and commitment one has toward their spiritual journey. When personal choices are guided by discipline, they not only enhance personal integrity but also contribute to the development of virtues such as patience, resilience, and inner strength—all of which are essential for spiritual well-being.

Empathy and **compassion** are central to the connection between personal choices and spiritual well-being. Choices that reflect kindness and consideration for others—whether other humans, animals, or the environment—nurture a sense of interconnectedness and foster a deeper understanding of the shared experience of life. By making choices that prioritize the well-being of others, individuals strengthen their own spiritual growth. For example, the decision to support fair trade products or to reduce one's environmental impact can enhance spiritual well-being by fostering a sense of responsibility for the larger world and its inhabitants. This outward focus, where personal actions are aligned with the good of others, helps cultivate a greater sense of unity, compassion, and moral fulfillment.

Service to others is another area where personal choices directly impact spiritual well-being. Acts of service, whether through volunteering, helping others in need, or offering support to one's community, are powerful ways of connecting personal actions with spiritual growth. These choices not only contribute to the well-being of others but also reinforce the values of generosity, selflessness, and compassion that are central to many spiritual paths. By making choices that involve giving time, resources, or effort to help others, individuals experience a deep sense of purpose and spiritual nourishment. Service becomes a means of transcending the self and contributing to something larger, fostering both personal fulfillment and a connection to the collective good.

Non-attachment, a key concept in spiritual traditions like Buddhism and Stoicism, also reflects how personal choices impact spiritual well-being. By making choices that reflect non-attachment to material possessions, status, or fleeting desires, individuals cultivate inner freedom and peace. Choosing simplicity, moderation, or detachment from materialism helps reduce the suffering that comes from clinging to impermanent things. This, in turn, enhances spiritual well-being by promoting contentment and inner tranquility. Personal choices that prioritize non-attachment lead to a deeper sense of satisfaction, as they align with the spiritual goal of overcoming desire and attachment to the material world.

Ultimately, the connection between personal choices and spiritual well-being lies in the **intention** behind each decision. When individuals approach their lives with the intention of acting in harmony with their spiritual values, they cultivate a sense of purpose, integrity, and inner peace. Every decision—no matter how small—becomes an opportunity to practice the principles of one's spiritual path, whether that involves kindness, self-control, mindfulness, or service. These choices, made with awareness and intentionality, not only shape external outcomes but also have a profound impact on the internal landscape, fostering a sense of fulfillment, purpose, and spiritual alignment.

In conclusion, the personal choices individuals make on a daily basis are powerful reflections of their spiritual journey. These choices, when made in alignment with one's values and beliefs, contribute to a deeper sense of well-being, inner peace, and connection to the larger world. By living intentionally and with a commitment to ethical and mindful decision-making, individuals enhance their spiritual growth and create a life that resonates with their highest ideals. Through this continuous practice, personal choices become a source of spiritual nourishment, fostering both individual and collective well-being.

Chapter 6: Stoicism – Mastering the Self Through Reason

Stoicism, an ancient philosophy born in the heart of Greece and refined in Rome, offers a powerful framework for mastering the self through reason, discipline, and emotional resilience. At its core, Stoicism teaches that while external events may be beyond human control, how one responds to these events is entirely within the individual's power. It is a philosophy that emphasizes self-sufficiency, urging individuals to cultivate inner strength, emotional stability, and rational thinking to navigate life's inevitable challenges.

For Stoics, the pursuit of spiritual and emotional well-being is rooted in the mastery of the self. Rather than being swayed by desires, fears, or external circumstances, the Stoic seeks to maintain equanimity and clarity of thought in every situation. By focusing on what can be controlled—one's own actions, thoughts, and reactions—the Stoic philosophy offers a pathway to achieving peace of mind and personal freedom from the turbulence of life.

Central to Stoicism is the practice of self-discipline, which helps individuals manage their impulses and maintain a sense of balance. Whether facing success or failure, pleasure or pain, Stoicism teaches that life's challenges should be accepted with grace and a calm mind. The Stoic approach is not to deny the reality of hardship but to embrace it as an opportunity for growth and self-mastery, understanding that suffering and joy are transient experiences shaped by one's own perceptions.

This chapter explores the key tenets of Stoicism, focusing on how self-discipline, reason, and acceptance form the foundation of spiritual and emotional resilience. It will illustrate how Stoicism serves as a practical guide for living a life of purpose, helping individuals build inner strength and master the art of navigating life's complexities with wisdom and calm resolve. Through the Stoic lens, the path to fulfillment is not found in external success but in mastering the self and embracing the challenges life presents.

Stoic philosophy as a way to spiritual and emotional self-sufficiency

STOIC PHILOSOPHY, ORIGINATING in ancient Greece and further developed in Rome, offers a powerful framework for achieving spiritual and emotional self-sufficiency. At its core, Stoicism teaches that human beings can cultivate inner peace, resilience, and autonomy by focusing on what is within their control and letting go of concerns about things outside their control. This practical approach to life fosters a sense of personal mastery over one's thoughts, emotions, and actions, leading to a profound form of spiritual and emotional independence.

Central to Stoic thought is the distinction between what is in our control and what is not. The Stoics emphasized that the only things truly within our control are our own beliefs, attitudes, and responses to events. External circumstances—such as wealth, health, reputation, or the actions of others—are ultimately beyond our direct influence. Therefore, worrying or becoming attached to these external factors leads to unnecessary suffering and emotional turmoil. By accepting that we cannot control external outcomes, Stoicism encourages individuals to turn their attention inward, focusing on their reactions, decisions, and internal state. This shift toward self-mastery creates a foundation for spiritual and emotional self-sufficiency, as individuals learn to rely on their inner strength rather than on external validation or success.

Stoicism also places great emphasis on **virtue**, which is seen as the highest good. For the Stoics, living a virtuous life—one that aligns with wisdom, justice, courage, and temperance—brings true fulfillment and peace. Virtue is entirely within one's control, as it is based on the choices one makes in each moment. This focus on virtue helps individuals develop an inner moral compass, guiding them to act with integrity regardless of external circumstances. By cultivating virtue, Stoics are able to maintain emotional balance, even in the face of adversity, because their sense of worth and well-being is rooted in their character, not in outcomes or external approval. This grounding in virtue fosters emotional resilience and a deep sense of self-sufficiency, as individuals learn to navigate life with clarity and moral purpose.

Another key element of Stoicism is **emotional regulation**. The Stoics believed that destructive emotions, such as anger, fear, envy, and excessive desire, arise from faulty judgments about what is good or bad. By recognizing that external events are neutral and that emotional distress is the result of our interpretations, Stoicism teaches that we can train our minds to respond more rationally and calmly. This practice of emotional regulation is central to the Stoic path to spiritual and emotional self-sufficiency. Through self-discipline and mindfulness, Stoics learn to detach from emotions that cloud judgment or disrupt inner peace, instead cultivating an attitude of equanimity and acceptance.

One of the most famous Stoic exercises is the **premeditation of evils** (*premeditatio malorum*), in which individuals deliberately contemplate possible negative outcomes—such as loss, illness, or failure—so that they can mentally prepare for adversity. This practice is not meant to encourage pessimism, but rather to reduce the emotional shock and fear that often accompany unexpected challenges. By mentally rehearsing potential hardships, Stoics strengthen their emotional resilience and reinforce their ability to remain calm and composed in difficult situations. This mental preparedness contributes to emotional self-sufficiency, as individuals are less likely to be overwhelmed or destabilized by life's inevitable difficulties.

A significant aspect of Stoicism's spiritual dimension is its teaching on **acceptance of fate**, or *amor fati*—the love of one's fate. Stoics believe that everything that happens is part of the natural order, governed by universal reason or *logos*. By accepting the flow of events and embracing life as it unfolds, Stoics cultivate a sense of peace and harmony with the world. This acceptance does not imply passivity or resignation; rather, it encourages individuals to make the best of whatever circumstances arise, understanding that their true power lies in how they respond to those circumstances. This practice of acceptance deepens one's emotional self-sufficiency by fostering a mindset that is not dependent on things going "right," but is instead adaptable and resilient in the face of any outcome.

Detachment from external desires is another critical component of Stoic philosophy. The Stoics taught that attachment to wealth, fame, pleasure, or other external goods leads to emotional instability because these things are impermanent and beyond our control. By practicing detachment from external desires, Stoics free themselves from the anxiety, fear, and disappointment that often accompany the pursuit of material or social success. This detachment is not about rejecting life's pleasures, but about not being emotionally dependent on them. It allows individuals to enjoy what they have while maintaining inner freedom and peace, regardless of whether those external circumstances change. This inner independence is the cornerstone of Stoic self-sufficiency, as it empowers individuals to find contentment within themselves rather than in external achievements or possessions.

The Stoic approach to **death and mortality** further reinforces emotional and spiritual self-sufficiency. Stoics encourage regular contemplation of death as a way to develop a balanced perspective on life. By acknowledging the inevitability of death and accepting it as a natural part of existence, individuals can live more fully in the present, free from the fear of loss or the anxiety of the unknown. This acceptance of mortality fosters a sense of spiritual maturity and emotional clarity, as it helps individuals prioritize what truly matters—living virtuously and making the most of each moment—rather than clinging to the illusion of permanence. In this way, Stoicism offers a pathway to spiritual fulfillment through the acceptance of life's impermanence.

Stoicism also emphasizes the importance of **community and service** to others, which balances its focus on self-sufficiency with a sense of responsibility to the larger world. Stoics believe that all human beings are part of a larger whole, interconnected by their shared humanity and rational nature. While Stoicism teaches individuals to be self-reliant, it also encourages them to act with compassion and justice toward others. This sense of duty to the common good enriches one's spiritual and emotional life by fostering a sense of purpose and connection beyond the self. By contributing to the well-being of others, Stoics find meaning in their actions and deepen their sense of fulfillment, while maintaining their inner independence.

In conclusion, Stoic philosophy offers a powerful approach to achieving spiritual and emotional self-sufficiency. Through the cultivation of virtue, emotional regulation, detachment from external desires, and acceptance of life's uncertainties, Stoics develop an inner strength that allows them to navigate the challenges of life with resilience and grace. By focusing on what is within their control and living in alignment with their values, Stoics find fulfillment in their own actions and character, rather than in external outcomes. This focus on self-mastery and inner peace fosters a profound sense of independence, enabling individuals to live with both spiritual depth and emotional balance in an unpredictable world.

The importance of self-discipline and accepting life's challenges

SELF-DISCIPLINE IS a cornerstone of personal and spiritual development. It is the ability to exercise control over one's desires, impulses, and actions in pursuit of higher goals and values. The importance of self-discipline becomes especially clear when facing life's challenges, which often test an individual's resolve and character. In many philosophical and spiritual traditions, the cultivation of self-discipline is seen as essential for achieving inner peace, resilience, and long-term fulfillment. Through self-discipline, individuals can navigate hardships with grace and determination, transforming difficulties into opportunities for growth and self-mastery.

Self-discipline is not merely about restriction or deprivation; rather, it is the deliberate choice to prioritize actions that align with one's long-term values over short-term gratification. It requires the ability to delay immediate rewards, resist temptations, and focus on what truly matters in the pursuit of personal and spiritual goals. By practicing self-discipline, individuals gain greater control over their thoughts and behaviors, enabling them to act with purpose and intention rather than being driven by momentary impulses. This control fosters a sense of empowerment and clarity, as disciplined actions are grounded in a clear sense of direction and purpose.

Life inevitably presents challenges—whether in the form of personal setbacks, external circumstances, or emotional struggles. The ability to accept these challenges and face them with self-discipline is crucial for maintaining balance and resilience. Acceptance does not mean resignation or passive submission to adversity; instead, it involves acknowledging the reality of difficulties while maintaining the determination to respond constructively. By accepting life's challenges, individuals shift their focus from resisting or avoiding discomfort to confronting it head-on, using self-discipline to manage their emotions and make thoughtful decisions.

For example, when faced with disappointment, failure, or loss, self-discipline helps individuals maintain perspective and resist the urge to react impulsively or destructively. It allows them to pause, reflect, and choose actions that are in line with their higher values. This disciplined approach leads to greater emotional stability, as individuals are less likely to be overwhelmed by negative emotions or external events. Instead, they are able to navigate challenges with a sense of calm and resolve, knowing that they have the inner strength to face whatever comes their way.

The practice of self-discipline also strengthens one's ability to endure discomfort or hardship. Whether it is physical, emotional, or mental discomfort, self-discipline provides the fortitude to persist through difficulties without giving in to discouragement or defeat. This endurance is essential for personal growth, as it allows individuals to develop resilience and inner strength over time. Each time one chooses to persevere in the face of adversity, self-discipline is reinforced, building a foundation of confidence and self-reliance. Through this process, challenges become opportunities for honing one's character and deepening spiritual maturity.

In many spiritual and philosophical traditions, the importance of self-discipline is closely tied to the concept of **virtue** or living in alignment with one's highest principles. To live a virtuous life requires the ability to consistently act in accordance with values such as honesty, compassion, courage, and integrity. This consistency can only be achieved through the practice of self-discipline, as it takes effort and commitment to uphold one's values, especially in difficult circumstances. When challenges arise, it is easy to be swayed by fear, anger, or temptation, but self-discipline acts as a guiding force, ensuring that actions remain rooted in virtue and not in emotional reactivity.

Self-discipline also plays a key role in **personal responsibility**, which is another important aspect of accepting life's challenges. When individuals face difficulties, it can be tempting to blame external circumstances, other people, or even fate for their misfortunes. However, self-discipline encourages individuals to take responsibility for their own responses to challenges, recognizing that while they may not control what happens to them, they do control how they react. By accepting this responsibility, individuals reclaim their power to shape their lives and overcome adversity. This mindset shift is crucial for personal growth, as it empowers individuals to take proactive steps toward improvement and resilience, rather than becoming passive victims of circumstance.

Another important aspect of self-discipline is its role in cultivating **patience** and **perseverance**. Life's challenges are rarely resolved quickly or easily, and it is often through sustained effort and persistence that individuals achieve their goals or overcome obstacles. Self-discipline enables individuals to stay focused on long-term objectives, even when progress is slow or setbacks occur. This patience is essential for maintaining motivation and perspective, especially in the face of temporary frustrations or difficulties. By practicing self-discipline, individuals learn to embrace the process of growth and change, trusting that their efforts will lead to positive outcomes over time.

Acceptance of life's challenges also fosters **emotional resilience**. When individuals accept that challenges are an inevitable part of life, they are better equipped to cope with the stress and uncertainty that accompanies difficult situations. This acceptance allows them to approach challenges with a sense of calm and resolve, rather than becoming overwhelmed by anxiety or fear. By combining acceptance with self-discipline, individuals can navigate emotionally charged situations with clarity and focus, making decisions that align with their values and long-term goals. Emotional resilience, in turn, strengthens one's capacity to face future challenges with confidence and composure.

Furthermore, the practice of self-discipline leads to greater **self-awareness** and **mindfulness**. As individuals become more disciplined in their thoughts and actions, they develop a heightened awareness of their internal states—such as emotions, desires, and impulses. This mindfulness enables them to observe their reactions to challenges without becoming consumed by them, allowing for more thoughtful and deliberate responses. Self-discipline, therefore, acts as a bridge between mindfulness and action, helping individuals align their behavior with their deeper values and spiritual aspirations, even in the face of difficulty.

In conclusion, self-discipline and the acceptance of life's challenges are essential components of personal growth and spiritual well-being. Through self-discipline, individuals gain the inner strength and resilience needed to navigate adversity, while acceptance allows them to confront challenges with courage and composure. Together, these practices foster a sense of empowerment, integrity, and emotional balance, enabling individuals to live in alignment with their highest values and achieve long-term fulfillment. Life's challenges, rather than being obstacles to happiness, become opportunities for growth, transformation, and the deepening of one's character.

Chapter 7: Meditation and Mindfulness – The Inner Journey

Meditation and mindfulness are practices that transcend religious and cultural boundaries, offering individuals a powerful way to connect with their inner selves. These practices focus on cultivating presence, self-awareness, and inner peace, all without the need for divine beings or external forces. Instead, they guide individuals on a journey within, where the mind, body, and emotions are brought into harmony through disciplined awareness.

Across many spiritual traditions—whether rooted in Buddhism, secular mindfulness, or even Stoic practices—meditation serves as a tool for developing deeper insight into one's thoughts and feelings. By observing the mind's activity without attachment or judgment, individuals can develop a heightened sense of clarity, emotional resilience, and mental stillness. This process allows them to access their true selves, free from the distractions of everyday life or the noise of external influences.

Mindfulness, closely related to meditation, is the practice of bringing one's full attention to the present moment. Through mindful awareness, individuals can become more attuned to their thoughts, emotions, and physical sensations, fostering a deeper understanding of how their inner world shapes their experience of life. This awareness is not aimed at invoking divine guidance but rather at empowering the individual to take responsibility for their mental and emotional states.

This chapter explores how meditation and mindfulness practices from various traditions encourage self-awareness and personal growth, highlighting their role in fostering a deeper connection to the self. By emphasizing presence and the observation of the mind, these practices help individuals develop inner strength and emotional balance, providing a path to spiritual well-being that relies solely on personal discipline and introspection. Without the need for divine beings, meditation and mindfulness become tools for inner transformation and self-discovery, guiding individuals on a fulfilling journey within.

How meditation practices across traditions help individuals connect with their true selves

MEDITATION, IN ITS many forms, has been a cornerstone of spiritual practice across cultures and traditions for centuries. Whether in Buddhism, Hinduism, Taoism, or more secular modern mindfulness practices, meditation offers a path to self-discovery and inner awareness. At its core, meditation is a practice of stilling the mind and turning inward, allowing individuals to move beyond the surface-level distractions of daily life and connect with their true selves. Through consistent meditation, individuals are able to cultivate a deeper understanding of their thoughts, emotions, and behaviors, leading to greater self-awareness, clarity, and spiritual growth.

One of the key ways meditation helps individuals connect with their true selves is through the cultivation of **mindfulness.** Mindfulness, the practice of being fully present in the moment without judgment, is central to many forms of meditation. By focusing attention on the breath, bodily sensations, or a particular point of concentration, individuals learn to observe their thoughts and emotions without becoming entangled in them. This detached observation allows meditators to step back from their habitual thought patterns and gain insight into the deeper workings of their mind. Over time, this practice helps individuals distinguish between their reactive mind—often influenced by ego, fear, or desire—and their true self, which is grounded in peace and awareness.

In traditions such as **Buddhism**, meditation is viewed as the key to awakening or enlightenment. The goal of meditation is to recognize the impermanence of all things and to transcend the ego-driven attachments that cause suffering. Through practices like Vipassana (insight meditation), individuals cultivate awareness of their moment-to-moment experiences, observing the arising and passing of thoughts and emotions. This practice leads to the realization that the self, as commonly understood, is an illusion—there is no permanent, unchanging self. Instead, the true self is seen as pure awareness, free from attachment to thoughts, feelings, and external conditions. By connecting with this deeper awareness, individuals experience liberation from the constant fluctuations of the mind and find peace in simply being.

Similarly, in **Hinduism**, meditation plays a crucial role in self-realization and connecting with the divine self, or **Atman**. Practices like **Dhyana** (meditative concentration) and **Jnana Yoga** (the path of knowledge) are designed to help individuals transcend the illusions of the material world and recognize their true nature as Atman, the eternal, divine consciousness that is identical with Brahman, the universal soul. Through focused meditation, individuals learn to quiet the mind and detach from the distractions of the physical world, allowing them to perceive the deeper truth of their existence. In this state of heightened awareness, meditators come to understand that their true self is not the body, mind, or ego, but the infinite, timeless consciousness that connects all beings.

In more secular contexts, meditation practices such as **mindfulness meditation** or **transcendental meditation** help individuals achieve self-awareness and emotional balance. In these practices, the goal is often to cultivate a sense of calm, focus, and inner clarity, allowing individuals to better understand their thoughts, emotions, and reactions. By developing this self-awareness, individuals are able to identify patterns of behavior or thought that may be causing stress, anxiety, or dissatisfaction. Over time, meditation helps them break free from these unproductive patterns and fosters a deeper connection to their authentic selves—an aspect of themselves that is more aligned with their core values, desires, and sense of purpose.

Another aspect of how meditation fosters connection with the true self is its role in **emotional regulation**. Many individuals are driven by their emotions, often reacting impulsively or getting caught up in negative states of mind such as anger, fear, or sadness. Meditation teaches individuals to observe these emotions without being controlled by them. By developing the ability to sit with difficult emotions and thoughts without reacting, meditators gain a deeper understanding of where these feelings come from and what triggers them. This emotional insight allows them to respond to life's challenges with greater clarity and equanimity, ultimately leading to a more balanced and centered sense of self. The ability to regulate emotions through meditation is crucial for maintaining inner peace and staying connected to the true self, even in the face of external difficulties.

Transcendence is another important theme in many meditation practices. In both spiritual and secular traditions, meditation offers a way to move beyond the limitations of the ego and everyday concerns, allowing individuals to experience a deeper, more expansive state of being. In traditions like **Taoism**, meditation is seen as a way to align oneself with the natural flow of the Tao, the fundamental principle that underlies all existence. By emptying the mind and cultivating stillness, practitioners can connect with the Tao and experience a sense of unity with the cosmos. This transcendent experience is a direct connection with the true self, which is not separate from the world but an integral part of the larger whole.

Meditation also fosters a deep sense of **self-acceptance** and compassion, both of which are vital for connecting with the true self.

Through meditation, individuals are encouraged to observe themselves with kindness and non-judgment, recognizing that their thoughts, feelings, and experiences are part of the human condition. This compassionate awareness allows meditators to accept themselves as they are, without striving for perfection or becoming entangled in self-criticism. By embracing themselves fully, individuals cultivate a sense of inner peace and wholeness, which is key to connecting with the true self. This process of self-acceptance often leads to greater compassion for others as well, as meditators come to see the shared struggles and humanity in everyone they encounter.

In many ways, meditation acts as a mirror, reflecting back to individuals the truth of who they are beneath the layers of ego, societal conditioning, and emotional turbulence. By stripping away the distractions and noise of everyday life, meditation provides a space for individuals to connect with their most authentic selves—free from the external influences that often cloud their judgment or shape their behavior. This connection with the true self is not only a source of inner peace and clarity but also serves as a foundation for living a more intentional and meaningful life. When individuals are in tune with their true selves, they are better able to make decisions that align with their values and live in a way that reflects their deeper purpose.

Ultimately, meditation practices across traditions offer individuals a profound tool for self-discovery and spiritual growth. Whether through mindfulness, concentration, or transcendental practices, meditation helps individuals cultivate self-awareness, emotional regulation, and a deeper understanding of their true nature. By connecting with the true self through meditation, individuals are able to experience greater inner peace, authenticity, and fulfillment, leading to a more harmonious relationship with both themselves and the world around them.

The focus on presence and self-awareness

without reference to divine beings

IN MANY SPIRITUAL AND philosophical traditions, the path to inner peace, fulfillment, and self-realization does not rely on the intervention of divine beings or the belief in a higher power. Instead, these traditions emphasize the importance of cultivating presence and self-awareness as a means to connect with one's true self and achieve spiritual growth. This approach, which focuses on the here and now, encourages individuals to take responsibility for their own thoughts, actions, and emotional states, guiding them toward a deeper understanding of their own minds and hearts. By doing so, they achieve greater clarity, peace, and autonomy, free from the need for external validation or divine guidance.

At the heart of this philosophy is the practice of **presence**—being fully engaged in the present moment without being distracted by past regrets or future anxieties. Presence is not just about physical awareness of one's surroundings; it is about cultivating a state of mind that is completely attuned to what is happening right now. When individuals learn to be fully present, they gain the ability to observe their thoughts and emotions with clarity, without becoming overwhelmed by them. This awareness creates a space between stimulus and response, allowing for more thoughtful, intentional reactions rather than knee-jerk emotional responses. The ability to stay present is a powerful tool for self-awareness, as it encourages individuals to witness their inner world with curiosity and openness, rather than judgment or attachment.

Self-awareness is closely linked to presence, as it involves understanding one's own thoughts, emotions, desires, and behaviors on a deeper level. Self-awareness helps individuals recognize patterns in their thinking, identify the root causes of their emotions, and gain insight into how their beliefs and perceptions shape their experiences. This understanding allows individuals to act with greater intentionality, making choices that align with their values and true selves rather than being driven by unconscious habits or external influences. Through self-awareness, people can recognize when they are acting out of fear, desire, or ego, and choose a more balanced and thoughtful path forward.

In traditions like **Buddhism**, **Stoicism**, and **secular mindfulness practices**, the focus on presence and self-awareness is a means to transcend suffering and achieve a state of inner peace. These traditions teach that much of human suffering arises from attachment to desires, expectations, and external circumstances, all of which are constantly in flux and beyond our control. By cultivating self-awareness and practicing presence, individuals learn to detach from these fleeting concerns and focus on what is within their control—their own mind and behavior. This detachment leads to greater emotional resilience, as individuals are no longer enslaved by their desires or fears but instead find peace in the present moment.

The practice of **mindfulness** is a key tool in developing both presence and self-awareness. Mindfulness involves paying attention to the present moment without judgment, observing one's thoughts, sensations, and surroundings with a sense of openness and curiosity. Whether through meditation, mindful breathing, or simply paying closer attention to daily activities, mindfulness helps individuals slow down and become more aware of the inner workings of their mind. This heightened awareness fosters self-understanding and self-compassion, as individuals begin to see themselves more clearly and with greater acceptance. By practicing mindfulness, individuals can step out of the autopilot mode that often governs their thoughts and actions, making room for intentional and thoughtful choices.

In these non-theistic approaches, there is no need for a divine being to grant enlightenment or guide individuals to self-realization. Instead, the path to self-awareness and fulfillment is seen as a personal journey that each individual must undertake for themselves. The emphasis is on personal responsibility—recognizing that one's thoughts, emotions, and actions are within their control and that true change comes from within. This focus on self-mastery aligns with the idea that the answers to life's most profound questions lie not in external forces or divine intervention but in one's own ability to observe, reflect, and grow through self-awareness.

Another key element of presence and self-awareness is the practice of **acceptance**. Without the need for divine beings to dictate meaning or purpose, individuals who practice presence learn to accept life as it is—both its joys and its challenges. This acceptance is not passive resignation but a mindful acknowledgment of reality. It allows individuals to release the struggle against what cannot be changed and to focus their energy on responding to life's circumstances with clarity and calm. In this sense, presence and self-awareness help individuals find peace in the present moment, regardless of external conditions, because they are no longer reliant on outside forces to define their experience.

Emotional regulation also plays a significant role in this process. Through presence and self-awareness, individuals develop the ability to recognize and manage their emotional reactions in real-time. Rather than being swept away by anger, fear, or anxiety, they learn to observe these emotions without identifying with them. This practice creates a sense of emotional stability and reduces the tendency to react impulsively. Over time, this emotional regulation fosters a deeper sense of inner peace, as individuals are no longer controlled by their emotions but can respond thoughtfully to whatever arises in their lives.

In addition, the focus on self-awareness and presence encourages individuals to **connect with their true selves**—the part of themselves that exists beyond societal expectations, ego-driven desires, or external labels. By stripping away these layers through mindful self-reflection, individuals come to understand who they truly are at their core. This connection to the true self leads to a greater sense of authenticity and fulfillment, as individuals begin to live in alignment with their deepest values and beliefs. Presence allows them to engage with life from this authentic place, responding to challenges and opportunities with wisdom and integrity.

In **secular practices**, the absence of a belief in divine beings does not diminish the depth of spiritual experience. Instead, it shifts the focus inward, emphasizing personal growth, self-discovery, and the cultivation of inner peace. These practices offer a way to explore the profound questions of existence—such as the nature of self, purpose, and meaning—through direct experience and introspection rather than through faith in external entities. By focusing on presence and self-awareness, individuals can access the same deep sense of connection and fulfillment that many seek through religious or spiritual means, but without the need for a divine intermediary.

Ultimately, the focus on presence and self-awareness without reference to divine beings is a powerful approach to personal growth and spiritual well-being. It places the individual at the center of their own journey, empowering them to take responsibility for their thoughts, emotions, and actions. Through the cultivation of mindfulness, acceptance, and emotional regulation, individuals are able to connect with their true selves and find peace in the present moment. This self-awareness fosters a deeper sense of clarity, purpose, and fulfillment, allowing individuals to navigate life's complexities with greater wisdom and grace, free from the need for external validation or divine guidance.

Chapter 8: Yoga – The Union of Body, Mind, and Self

Yoga is often associated with physical postures and exercises, but its true essence lies far beyond the physical practice. Rooted in ancient spiritual traditions, yoga is a holistic path that seeks to unite the body, mind, and self in the pursuit of inner peace, self-mastery, and spiritual fulfillment. It is a discipline that guides individuals toward harmony within themselves and with the world around them, focusing on the balance between physical, mental, and emotional well-being.

At its core, yoga emphasizes self-discipline and inner transformation. Through the practice of physical postures (asanas), breathing exercises (pranayama), and meditation, individuals are encouraged to cultivate a deep awareness of their own body and mind. This awareness extends beyond mere physical health; it is about achieving mastery over one's thoughts, emotions, and desires. The ultimate goal is to bring the self into a state of balance and tranquility, free from the distractions and attachments that often dominate daily life.

Yoga philosophy teaches that true spiritual growth comes from this union of the body and mind. It is through this integration that individuals can achieve a deeper sense of self-awareness, emotional resilience, and inner peace. Yoga is not a practice that requires divine worship or belief in a higher power; rather, it is a path of personal growth that empowers individuals to take responsibility for their own spiritual journey.

This chapter delves into the spiritual dimensions of yoga, exploring how it serves as a tool for self-mastery and inner peace. It highlights the discipline involved in yoga practice, showing how the union of body, mind, and self allows individuals to access deeper levels of spiritual fulfillment. By going beyond the physical, yoga becomes a path toward true balance, where the individual can experience a profound connection to themselves and the world around them.

Exploring the spiritual aspects of yoga beyond physical exercise

YOGA IS OFTEN ASSOCIATED with physical postures and fitness routines, but its true essence extends far beyond the physical body. Rooted in ancient Indian spiritual traditions, yoga is a holistic practice that seeks to unite the mind, body, and spirit in the pursuit of inner peace, self-awareness, and personal transformation. While the physical postures (*asanas*) are an important component, they are only one part of a much broader spiritual path that involves self-discipline, meditation, ethical living, and the cultivation of mindfulness. Exploring the spiritual aspects of yoga reveals a rich tradition that offers profound insights into the nature of the self and the journey toward inner harmony.

At the heart of yoga's spiritual dimension is the concept of **union**. The word "yoga" itself means union or to yoke, symbolizing the integration of the individual self with the universal consciousness. This union is not just about aligning the physical body with breath but also about harmonizing the mind, emotions, and spirit. Through yoga, individuals aim to transcend the ego and the distractions of the material world, connecting with a deeper, more authentic aspect of themselves. This sense of union fosters a feeling of oneness with the universe, encouraging practitioners to see themselves as part of something greater than their individual identities.

One of the key spiritual elements of yoga is **self-realization**. Yoga is a tool for exploring the true nature of the self, beyond the layers of ego, societal conditioning, and mental noise. Through practices such as meditation, breath control (*pranayama*), and introspection, yoga encourages individuals to quiet the mind and look inward, cultivating a deeper awareness of their inner being. This process of self-inquiry leads to greater clarity about one's true nature, often described in yogic philosophy as the eternal, unchanging self (*Atman*), which exists beyond the physical body and mental fluctuations. The journey of yoga is ultimately a journey of awakening to this deeper, spiritual reality.

Mindfulness and presence are also central to the spiritual practice of yoga. The emphasis on connecting breath with movement in asanas is designed to bring practitioners fully into the present moment. This mindfulness extends beyond the physical practice and into everyday life, encouraging individuals to live with greater awareness, intentionality, and focus. By cultivating presence, yoga helps individuals break free from the constant mental chatter and distractions that often dominate the mind. This mindful awareness creates space for deeper reflection, allowing practitioners to observe their thoughts, emotions, and reactions without becoming entangled in them. Through this process, individuals gain insight into their habitual patterns and learn to live with greater consciousness and compassion.

In addition to mindfulness, yoga teaches **self-discipline** as a means of spiritual growth. The ethical guidelines of yoga, known as the *Yamas* and *Niyamas*, offer a framework for living a balanced and virtuous life. The *Yamas* are five moral precepts that govern one's interactions with others: non-violence (*ahimsa*), truthfulness (*satya*), non-stealing (*asteya*), sexual restraint (*brahmacharya*), and non-attachment (*aparigraha*). The *Niyamas* are five internal disciplines that focus on personal growth and self-care, including cleanliness (*saucha*), contentment (*santosha*), self-discipline (*tapas*), self-study (*svadhyaya*), and surrender to a higher power (*Ishvara pranidhana*). Together, these ethical guidelines provide a roadmap for living in harmony with oneself and others, supporting both personal and spiritual development.

The practice of **meditation** is another key component of yoga's spiritual aspect. Meditation allows practitioners to still the mind and connect with their inner consciousness, fostering a sense of inner peace and clarity. It is through meditation that the deeper layers of the self are revealed, allowing individuals to move beyond surface-level thoughts and emotions. In traditional yoga, meditation is often considered the pinnacle of the practice, as it helps individuals achieve the ultimate goal of *moksha*, or liberation from the cycle of suffering and rebirth. By cultivating a meditative mind, individuals can transcend the limitations of the ego and experience a deeper, more expansive state of awareness.

Breath control, or *pranayama*, is another spiritual tool in yoga that goes beyond its physical benefits. In yogic philosophy, the breath is seen as the bridge between the body and mind, and mastering the breath is key to mastering the mind. *Pranayama* involves a series of controlled breathing exercises that help regulate the flow of energy (*prana*) within the body, promoting balance and mental clarity. By controlling the breath, practitioners can calm the nervous system, reduce stress, and enhance concentration, allowing for deeper meditation and spiritual insight. The breath is not just a physiological process in yoga; it is a sacred tool for aligning the mind and body with the higher self.

The **spiritual philosophy** of yoga also encompasses the idea of **non-attachment** (*vairagya*). In yoga, practitioners are encouraged to detach from the outcomes of their efforts, recognizing that true peace comes from within, not from external circumstances. This principle of non-attachment helps individuals let go of the need for external validation, success, or material gain, instead focusing on cultivating inner contentment and equanimity. Non-attachment is particularly relevant in modern life, where many people are driven by external achievements and social pressures. By practicing non-attachment, yoga teaches that inner peace and fulfillment are found by looking inward rather than outward.

Yoga's spiritual dimension is also deeply connected to the idea of **service** or **selfless action** (*karma yoga*). In karma yoga, individuals are encouraged to act without attachment to the fruits of their labor, offering their work as an act of devotion and service to others. This form of yoga emphasizes the importance of humility, generosity, and compassion in daily life, reminding practitioners that their spiritual growth is not separate from their actions in the world. By serving others with a pure heart, without seeking recognition or reward, individuals cultivate a sense of unity with all beings, reinforcing the idea that yoga is not just a personal practice but a way of living in harmony with the greater whole.

Ultimately, yoga is a **spiritual journey** that extends far beyond the physical benefits of flexibility and strength. It is a path of self-discovery, mindfulness, and transformation that leads individuals to a deeper understanding of their true nature and their place in the universe. Through the practice of asanas, meditation, breath control, and ethical living, yoga offers a comprehensive system for cultivating spiritual awareness and inner peace. By integrating these spiritual aspects into their practice, individuals can move beyond the limitations of the physical body and connect with the deeper, more profound aspects of their being, leading to a life of greater balance, fulfillment, and harmony.

The role of self-mastery, discipline, and inner peace in yoga philosophy

IN THE PHILOSOPHY OF yoga, self-mastery, discipline, and inner peace are central to achieving a life of balance, fulfillment, and spiritual growth. Yoga is not merely a physical practice but a holistic system that emphasizes the cultivation of mental, emotional, and spiritual well-being through dedicated effort and self-control. These core principles guide practitioners on a journey toward greater self-awareness, enabling them to transcend the distractions and obstacles of everyday life and connect with their true selves. The pursuit of self-mastery and inner peace is a gradual process that requires continuous practice, reflection, and discipline, but it is ultimately the key to achieving lasting fulfillment and harmony.

Self-mastery in yoga is the ability to control and understand one's thoughts, emotions, desires, and reactions. It is about learning to observe the fluctuations of the mind without becoming entangled in them. In this sense, self-mastery is a practice of mindfulness—being aware of how the mind works and developing the ability to choose how to respond, rather than reacting impulsively. Through consistent practice of asanas (physical postures), meditation, and pranayama (breath control), yoga teaches individuals to quiet the mind and remain present, even in challenging situations. This mental clarity allows practitioners to maintain balance and composure, no matter what circumstances arise, and leads to greater self-control over emotions and behaviors.

Achieving self-mastery requires **discipline**, both on and off the mat. Discipline in yoga, or *tapas*, refers to the inner fire and commitment needed to pursue the practice regularly and with intention. It is the willingness to do the work, to show up for oneself, and to persevere, even when faced with obstacles or discomfort. Whether it is maintaining a regular meditation practice, committing to a healthy lifestyle, or following the ethical principles outlined in the Yamas and Niyamas, discipline is essential for making progress on the yogic path. It is through discipline that individuals can develop the strength and resilience needed to overcome the challenges that arise on the journey to self-mastery.

Yoga recognizes that the mind and body are deeply interconnected, and the practice of physical discipline through the asanas is a way to cultivate mental discipline as well. By holding challenging postures and breathing deeply through discomfort, practitioners learn to remain calm and focused, training the mind to remain steady even in the face of difficulty. This physical discipline mirrors the mental and emotional discipline needed to navigate life's challenges with grace. The strength, flexibility, and balance developed on the mat are metaphors for the resilience, adaptability, and emotional balance needed in everyday life.

Discipline in yoga also extends to ethical living. The Yamas (moral restraints) and Niyamas (observances) provide a framework for living a life of integrity and self-discipline. The Yamas include principles such as non-violence (ahimsa), truthfulness (satya), and non-attachment (aparigraha), which guide how individuals interact with the world around them. The Niyamas focus on self-discipline and personal growth, including practices like cleanliness (saucha), contentment (santosha), and self-study (svadhyaya). These ethical guidelines are designed to purify both the mind and body, fostering a life of balance and harmony that supports the deeper spiritual goals of yoga.

The practice of self-mastery and discipline naturally leads to the cultivation of **inner peace**, a central goal of yoga. Inner peace is the result of mastering one's thoughts, emotions, and reactions, so that external events no longer have the power to disturb the mind. By practicing yoga with discipline, individuals learn to cultivate an inner state of calm that remains stable even in the midst of external chaos. This inner peace arises from the understanding that true happiness and fulfillment come from within, not from external circumstances. As practitioners deepen their connection with their true selves through yoga, they learn to let go of attachments, desires, and fears that cause suffering, allowing them to experience a profound sense of contentment and peace.

In yoga philosophy, **meditation** plays a crucial role in cultivating both self-mastery and inner peace. Through meditation, individuals practice quieting the mind, observing their thoughts without attachment, and connecting with their inner consciousness. Over time, this practice helps to dissolve the mental clutter and emotional turmoil that often dominate the mind, allowing individuals to access deeper states of peace and clarity. Meditation helps to strengthen the mind's ability to remain calm and focused, even in difficult situations, and supports the development of self-mastery by teaching individuals to respond to life's challenges with greater wisdom and equanimity.

Breath control, or pranayama, is another important tool for achieving self-mastery and inner peace in yoga. The breath is considered the bridge between the body and the mind, and by controlling the breath, practitioners can regulate their emotional and mental states. Techniques like deep, rhythmic breathing help calm the nervous system, reduce stress, and bring the mind into a state of focus and tranquility. Through pranayama, individuals learn to use the breath as a tool to manage their emotions, quiet the mind, and maintain inner balance, even in the face of external challenges. This mastery over the breath is key to cultivating both self-discipline and inner peace.

Yoga's ultimate goal is **liberation**, or *moksha*, which is achieved through the mastery of the self and the cultivation of inner peace. As individuals practice yoga with discipline, they gradually shed the layers of ego, attachment, and desire that bind them to suffering. Through self-mastery, they learn to let go of the mental and emotional patterns that cause pain, and through inner peace, they find the freedom to live authentically and with purpose. Yoga teaches that true liberation comes not from external success or material gain but from within—through the mastery of one's own mind and the cultivation of a deep sense of inner peace.

In conclusion, self-mastery, discipline, and inner peace are fundamental principles in yoga philosophy that guide practitioners toward a life of balance, fulfillment, and spiritual awakening. Through dedicated practice and self-discipline, individuals develop the strength and resilience needed to face life's challenges with grace. As they cultivate self-mastery, they gain greater control over their thoughts, emotions, and actions, allowing them to live with greater intention and purpose. This journey ultimately leads to inner peace, as individuals learn to find contentment and fulfillment from within, free from the distractions and attachments of the external world. Yoga, therefore, offers a path to both personal transformation and spiritual liberation, grounded in the principles of discipline, self-mastery, and peace.

Chapter 9: Personal Growth as Spiritual Practice

In the modern world, the lines between personal growth, psychology, and spirituality are often blurred, with many individuals finding deep spiritual fulfillment through the pursuit of self-improvement and emotional healing. Personal growth movements, often grounded in psychological insights, emphasize self-awareness, resilience, and the importance of emotional well-being. While these approaches are secular in nature, they share many elements traditionally associated with spiritual practice—such as self-reflection, the cultivation of inner peace, and the pursuit of a meaningful life.

Self-help philosophies encourage individuals to confront their fears, desires, and emotional wounds, using techniques such as mindfulness, journaling, and goal-setting to achieve personal transformation. These processes can feel deeply spiritual, as they involve a commitment to self-discovery and healing, helping individuals align with their true selves. In many ways, this focus on personal development becomes a form of spiritual work, where the journey inward reveals not just emotional health but also deeper truths about one's purpose and existence.

Self-care, too, is more than just a routine for maintaining physical and mental health—it can be an act of self-compassion and spiritual nurturing. By taking the time to care for oneself, individuals create space for healing and growth, allowing them to connect with their inner world in profound ways. In this sense, self-care is both a practical and spiritual practice, helping individuals cultivate peace and balance in their lives.

This chapter explores how personal growth movements and self-help practices incorporate spiritual dimensions, highlighting the ways in which emotional healing and self-care serve as modern forms of spiritual work. It reveals how the pursuit of self-improvement can lead to greater inner peace and purpose, offering individuals a path to spiritual fulfillment through their own growth and transformation. By integrating psychology with spiritual practice, personal development becomes a journey toward wholeness and self-awareness, where emotional and spiritual well-being are deeply intertwined.

How self-help, psychology, and personal growth movements integrate spiritual dimensions

IN RECENT DECADES, the fields of self-help, psychology, and personal growth have increasingly incorporated spiritual dimensions into their frameworks, offering individuals a more holistic approach to personal development. While these movements often begin with a focus on improving mental health, emotional well-being, and life satisfaction, many of them recognize that true fulfillment requires more than just addressing psychological needs. They explore the deeper aspects of human existence—purpose, meaning, connection, and inner peace—blurring the lines between personal growth and spirituality. By integrating spiritual principles, these movements help individuals not only achieve external success but also cultivate inner harmony and self-realization.

One of the key ways in which self-help and personal growth movements integrate spirituality is through the focus on **self-awareness** and the pursuit of a higher purpose. Many self-help methodologies encourage individuals to look beyond material achievements or societal definitions of success and instead focus on what brings true meaning and fulfillment. This often involves self-reflection and mindfulness practices that encourage people to explore their inner worlds—their values, beliefs, and motivations. By becoming more self-aware, individuals can identify what truly matters to them, often leading to a greater sense of purpose that transcends superficial goals.

Incorporating spiritual dimensions into personal growth also emphasizes the importance of **self-transcendence**—the idea that fulfillment comes not only from personal achievements but also from contributing to something greater than oneself. Self-help literature frequently encourages individuals to move beyond ego-driven desires, such as status or material wealth, and instead focus on how they can serve others, contribute to their communities, or connect with a higher cause. This aligns with spiritual traditions that emphasize service, compassion, and altruism as paths to self-realization. By integrating these values, personal growth movements help individuals find deeper meaning and satisfaction by fostering a sense of connection to the world around them.

The rise of **mindfulness** and **meditation** practices in psychology and personal growth is another example of how these fields integrate spiritual dimensions. Originally rooted in Buddhist and Eastern spiritual traditions, mindfulness has been adapted into mainstream psychological approaches as a tool for managing stress, anxiety, and emotional regulation. However, beyond its therapeutic benefits, mindfulness offers a spiritual dimension by encouraging individuals to cultivate presence, awareness, and non-attachment. Through mindfulness, individuals learn to observe their thoughts and emotions without being controlled by them, fostering a sense of inner calm and clarity. This practice leads to a deeper connection with the present moment, often considered a spiritual state where one can experience a greater sense of peace and contentment.

Many personal growth movements also draw on the concept of **inner transformation**, which is often linked to spiritual awakening. Books, workshops, and seminars on self-improvement frequently discuss the need for individuals to undergo a deep inner shift in order to unlock their full potential. This transformation is not just about changing behaviors or achieving goals, but about evolving one's consciousness—letting go of limiting beliefs, old patterns, and emotional baggage that no longer serve one's higher self. This process mirrors spiritual teachings that emphasize self-purification, enlightenment, and the transcendence of the ego. By framing personal growth as a journey of inner transformation, these movements highlight the spiritual dimension of self-improvement, where the ultimate goal is not just external success but inner peace and self-realization.

The integration of **positive psychology** with spirituality has also become a significant trend in recent years. Positive psychology focuses on fostering strengths, well-being, and fulfillment, rather than just treating mental illness. It emphasizes the development of qualities such as gratitude, compassion, forgiveness, and resilience—all of which are central to many spiritual traditions. By encouraging individuals to cultivate these virtues, positive psychology helps people not only improve their emotional well-being but also develop a more profound sense of connection to others and the world around them. These practices often lead to a greater appreciation for life's inherent beauty and a deeper sense of meaning, which are spiritual experiences in themselves.

Incorporating spiritual dimensions into personal growth movements also involves addressing the **mind-body connection**. Many self-help and psychological approaches now acknowledge that mental and emotional well-being cannot be fully achieved without also considering the health of the body. Practices such as yoga, breathwork, and energy healing, which have roots in spiritual traditions, are increasingly being incorporated into personal development programs. These practices emphasize the idea that the body is a vessel for spiritual growth and that by caring for the body through movement, breath, and energy balance, individuals can enhance their mental clarity and emotional stability. The integration of mind-body practices into personal growth fosters a more holistic understanding of well-being, where physical, mental, and spiritual health are interconnected.

The concept of **personal responsibility** is another way in which self-help movements align with spiritual principles. Many personal growth teachings emphasize that individuals have the power to shape their own lives through their choices, attitudes, and beliefs. This idea is closely related to spiritual teachings on self-mastery and free will, where individuals are seen as co-creators of their reality. Personal responsibility involves taking ownership of one's thoughts, emotions, and actions, recognizing that the path to personal and spiritual fulfillment requires conscious effort and intention. By embracing this principle, individuals are empowered to take control of their own growth, both in terms of external success and inner development.

Visualization and **affirmations**, common tools in self-help and personal growth, also have spiritual undertones. Visualization involves mentally imagining a desired outcome or state of being, while affirmations are positive statements used to reprogram the subconscious mind. Both practices are based on the belief that thoughts and intentions have the power to shape reality, an idea that is rooted in spiritual traditions such as the Law of Attraction or various forms of energy healing. By using these tools, individuals are encouraged to focus not only on external goals but also on cultivating a mindset that aligns with their highest aspirations, reinforcing the spiritual dimension of personal growth.

Moreover, the rise of **spiritual psychology**, a field that blends traditional psychology with spiritual wisdom, illustrates how the integration of these two realms can lead to more profound healing and growth. Spiritual psychology encourages individuals to view their life challenges as opportunities for spiritual development and to approach mental and emotional healing from a holistic perspective. It emphasizes that personal growth is not just about resolving psychological issues but about awakening to a deeper understanding of the self and one's place in the universe. This approach to psychology fosters a greater sense of purpose, connection, and inner peace, aligning personal growth with spiritual awakening.

In conclusion, the integration of spiritual dimensions into self-help, psychology, and personal growth movements provides individuals with a more comprehensive and meaningful approach to personal development. By focusing on self-awareness, inner transformation, mindfulness, and connection to a higher purpose, these movements help people move beyond superficial goals and embrace a deeper, more spiritual journey toward fulfillment. The blending of psychology with spiritual practices creates a path that nurtures not only the mind and emotions but also the soul, fostering a sense of wholeness, purpose, and peace that transcends the ordinary experience of personal growth. Through this integration, individuals can experience profound personal transformation that encompasses both inner and outer success.

The practice of self-care and emotional healing as spiritual work

SELF-CARE AND EMOTIONAL healing have traditionally been viewed as practices aimed at improving mental and physical well-being, but they also hold deep spiritual significance. In many spiritual traditions and modern personal growth philosophies, the journey toward inner peace and enlightenment begins with nurturing the self—attending to emotional wounds, creating space for healing, and fostering self-compassion. Far from being acts of selfishness, self-care and emotional healing are considered essential steps in aligning with one's true self, enhancing spiritual growth, and cultivating a sense of wholeness. When approached with intention and mindfulness, these practices become powerful spiritual work that connects individuals to their inner source of strength, clarity, and peace.

At its core, **self-care** involves making deliberate choices that support one's overall well-being. While it often includes activities like physical exercise, proper nutrition, rest, and relaxation, self-care extends beyond the physical body. It encompasses nurturing the mind and spirit by creating balance, reducing stress, and fostering inner peace. When self-care is viewed through a spiritual lens, it becomes a practice of honoring the body as a sacred vessel and the mind as a tool for self-awareness. By prioritizing self-care, individuals demonstrate reverence for their own existence and acknowledge that they are worthy of love, attention, and care.

Self-care is a spiritual practice because it helps cultivate **mindfulness and presence**—key elements in many spiritual paths. When individuals make time for self-care, they are invited to slow down and become more attuned to their inner experience. Whether it's through meditation, mindful breathing, or simply pausing to reflect on one's needs, self-care fosters a greater sense of presence and connection to the moment. This presence allows individuals to listen to their body and emotions, understanding what they need to feel balanced, nourished, and whole. By being mindful of these needs, individuals can align their actions with their inner truth, which is a deeply spiritual act of self-awareness and self-honoring.

Emotional healing, on the other hand, involves addressing the inner wounds and unresolved feelings that may be blocking one's ability to experience joy, peace, or connection. Emotional wounds can stem from past traumas, negative experiences, or unprocessed feelings such as grief, anger, or fear. From a spiritual perspective, healing these wounds is not only about achieving emotional stability but also about releasing the emotional and energetic burdens that prevent individuals from living fully and authentically. Emotional healing allows individuals to free themselves from patterns of pain and suffering, creating space for love, compassion, and spiritual growth.

In many spiritual traditions, the process of emotional healing is seen as a journey of **self-discovery and transformation**. It involves confronting difficult emotions, understanding the root causes of suffering, and learning to let go of attachments to past experiences that no longer serve the individual. This journey requires courage and vulnerability, as it often involves facing the parts of oneself that have been suppressed or ignored. By engaging in this deep emotional work, individuals can integrate their experiences, find meaning in their struggles, and transform their pain into wisdom and strength. This process of integration is a form of spiritual alchemy, turning emotional wounds into opportunities for personal and spiritual evolution.

Self-compassion is a key element in both self-care and emotional healing, and it is essential for viewing these practices as spiritual work. In many spiritual teachings, compassion for others is emphasized as a way to foster love, empathy, and connection. However, self-compassion—being kind and gentle with oneself in times of difficulty—is equally important. When individuals practice self-compassion, they create an environment of inner safety, where they can acknowledge their emotions, imperfections, and struggles without judgment or criticism. This self-kindness opens the door to healing, as it allows individuals to accept themselves fully and work through their challenges with patience and understanding. Cultivating self-compassion is a deeply spiritual act, as it reflects the divine truth that all beings, including oneself, are deserving of love and care.

Emotional healing is also tied to the concept of **release and forgiveness**, both of which are central to spiritual growth. Holding onto anger, resentment, or guilt can create energetic and emotional blockages that prevent individuals from experiencing peace and freedom. Forgiving oneself and others is an act of spiritual liberation, as it allows individuals to release the heavy burden of the past and open their hearts to new possibilities. This act of letting go is not about condoning harm or forgetting pain, but about freeing oneself from the grip of negative emotions that limit one's ability to grow and evolve. Through forgiveness, individuals can reclaim their power and move forward on their spiritual path with a sense of lightness and peace.

In many ways, the practice of self-care and emotional healing mirrors the spiritual journey of **self-mastery**. Just as spiritual seekers strive to transcend ego-driven desires and align with their higher selves, individuals engaged in self-care and healing work strive to transcend the emotional and psychological patterns that cause suffering. By caring for themselves with intention and healing their emotional wounds, individuals gain greater clarity, strength, and resilience. They learn to trust their inner wisdom and develop the emotional tools necessary to navigate life's challenges with grace. This mastery over one's inner world is a key aspect of spiritual development, as it fosters a deep sense of self-awareness, balance, and inner peace.

Furthermore, self-care and emotional healing cultivate a sense of **wholeness**, which is a fundamental aspect of spiritual well-being. Many spiritual traditions teach that individuals are inherently whole and complete, but that this sense of wholeness can become obscured by life's challenges, emotional wounds, or societal conditioning. Through self-care and healing, individuals reconnect with this inherent wholeness by nurturing all aspects of their being—physical, mental, emotional, and spiritual. This integration of the self fosters a sense of inner alignment, where individuals feel connected to their true selves and at peace with who they are. This wholeness is the foundation for living a spiritually fulfilling life, as it allows individuals to live authentically and in harmony with their highest purpose.

The spiritual aspect of self-care and emotional healing is also reflected in the concept of **balance**. In yoga, Eastern philosophies, and holistic health practices, balance is seen as essential for well-being and spiritual growth. By practicing self-care, individuals create balance in their lives by making space for rest, reflection, and rejuvenation. Emotional healing, similarly, brings balance to the heart and mind, allowing individuals to release emotional pain and restore a sense of harmony within. This balance is not just about avoiding extremes, but about living in a way that honors all aspects of the self—body, mind, and spirit. Through this balance, individuals find peace and clarity, which are essential for spiritual growth and connection.

Ultimately, self-care and emotional healing are integral to the spiritual journey because they foster a deeper connection to the self and the divine within. By prioritizing self-care, individuals honor their body, mind, and spirit as sacred, recognizing that they must nurture themselves in order to show up fully in the world. Emotional healing, in turn, allows individuals to release the burdens of the past and step into their true power, living from a place of authenticity, compassion, and inner peace. Together, these practices create a foundation for spiritual growth, as they enable individuals to live with greater intention, presence, and alignment with their higher purpose. Through self-care and healing, individuals embark on a profound journey of self-love, transformation, and spiritual awakening.

Chapter 10: Spirituality Without Borders – Global Movements

Across the globe, a growing number of spiritual movements are emerging that do not rely on theistic beliefs. These non-theistic traditions and practices are resonating with individuals who seek spiritual fulfillment without subscribing to a religion centered around divine beings. Whether rooted in ancient philosophies like Buddhism and Stoicism or found in modern mindfulness practices and secular humanism, these movements are gaining traction as they speak to a universal human desire for meaning, inner peace, and personal growth.

In today's highly interconnected and globalized world, the focus on self has become a dominant theme in both secular and spiritual contexts. With the widespread availability of information, people are exposed to a diverse array of spiritual teachings from different cultures and traditions. This exposure has led to the blending of ideas, where individuals pick and choose practices that resonate with them personally, often resulting in a spirituality that transcends national, religious, or cultural boundaries.

The global rise of non-theistic spiritual movements reflects a broader shift in values. In increasingly secular societies, people are turning inward, focusing on self-awareness, ethical living, and mental well-being as pathways to spiritual fulfillment. The emphasis on self is not viewed as selfishness but as a way to cultivate a more compassionate, connected, and meaningful existence—both individually and collectively.

This chapter explores the global rise of non-theistic spiritual movements, examining how these practices are spreading across borders and how they reflect a growing focus on self-realization in today's world. It will look at the role of globalization in fostering a more inclusive, flexible approach to spirituality—one that allows individuals to create their own spiritual paths without the need for divine worship or rigid religious structures. Through this lens, spirituality becomes not only a personal journey but also a global phenomenon, uniting people from diverse backgrounds in the pursuit of self-awareness and spiritual growth.

How non-theistic spiritual movements are growing worldwide

IN RECENT DECADES, there has been a noticeable rise in non-theistic spiritual movements across the globe, driven by a shift in how people relate to spirituality and organized religion. These movements, which do not rely on belief in a god or gods, instead emphasize personal growth, self-awareness, ethical living, and inner peace. The growth of these spiritual movements reflects a broader cultural trend in which individuals seek meaning and connection in ways that are not tied to traditional religious frameworks. As people increasingly explore alternative approaches to spirituality, non-theistic movements provide a space for personal transformation, mindfulness, and ethical practices that resonate with modern values and individual autonomy.

One of the primary reasons for the growth of non-theistic spiritual movements is the increasing **disillusionment with organized religion**. In many parts of the world, particularly in the West, people are moving away from traditional religious institutions due to a variety of factors, including perceived dogmatism, corruption, and a disconnect between institutional beliefs and contemporary social values. As a result, many individuals who still yearn for spiritual fulfillment are turning toward non-theistic practices that offer a sense of connection and purpose without the constraints of religious doctrine. These movements provide an alternative path for spiritual seekers who value autonomy and personal exploration over adherence to rigid belief systems.

Non-theistic spiritual movements also resonate with people seeking **inclusive and open-minded approaches to spirituality**. Traditional religions often come with a set of prescribed beliefs, rituals, and moral codes that may not align with modern progressive ideals, such as gender equality, LGBTQ+ rights, and environmentalism. In contrast, many non-theistic spiritual movements are more fluid and adaptable, allowing individuals to craft their own spiritual paths based on personal values and experiences. Movements such as secular humanism, mindfulness practices, and ethical veganism attract people who are interested in living a spiritually conscious life while embracing inclusivity, social justice, and compassion for all beings.

Another key factor contributing to the rise of non-theistic spiritual movements is the growing **popularity of mindfulness and meditation** practices. These practices, which originated in Eastern spiritual traditions such as Buddhism, have become mainstream across many cultures, particularly in secular contexts. Mindfulness, meditation, and yoga are now commonly practiced for their physical and mental health benefits, but they also provide a gateway to deeper spiritual exploration without the need for belief in a deity. For many individuals, these practices offer a form of spiritual connection through self-awareness, presence, and inner calm, aligning with their desire for a more personal and experiential approach to spirituality.

The emphasis on **self-realization and personal growth** within non-theistic spiritual movements also explains their increasing appeal. Many of these movements focus on the individual's journey toward self-discovery and inner fulfillment, encouraging personal responsibility for one's own spiritual development. Practices like journaling, mindfulness, and self-inquiry help individuals reflect on their thoughts, emotions, and behaviors, fostering a sense of self-awareness that contributes to spiritual well-being. This inward-focused approach allows individuals to take charge of their spiritual journeys, creating a deep sense of meaning and purpose that is not dependent on external religious authorities or supernatural beliefs.

The rise of **secular humanism** is another significant component of this global trend. Secular humanism emphasizes reason, ethics, and human dignity as the foundation for living a fulfilling life. It rejects the need for religious or supernatural explanations for morality and meaning, instead focusing on the capacity of human beings to create ethical systems and meaningful lives based on empathy, critical thinking, and social cooperation. Humanism appeals to individuals who are seeking a philosophy of life that respects human rights, promotes compassion, and encourages scientific inquiry, all while maintaining a commitment to personal and societal well-being. The spread of secular humanism has been facilitated by educational institutions, media, and global movements advocating for human rights, democracy, and rational thought.

Another factor driving the growth of non-theistic spiritual movements is the rise of **environmental awareness** and the search for more harmonious ways of living. Many individuals are increasingly aware of the environmental challenges facing the planet, such as climate change, deforestation, and species extinction. Non-theistic spiritual movements that emphasize connection to the Earth, nature, and sustainability—such as eco-spirituality and ethical veganism—offer a spiritual framework that aligns with these concerns. These movements encourage individuals to cultivate a deeper relationship with the natural world, recognizing the interconnectedness of all life and the ethical responsibility to protect and preserve the planet for future generations. For many, this form of spirituality provides a meaningful way to address ecological challenges while fostering a sense of spiritual connection and purpose.

Technology and the internet have also played a crucial role in the **global spread of non-theistic spiritual movements**. The digital age has made it easier than ever for people to access information, join online communities, and explore alternative spiritual practices. Platforms such as social media, podcasts, and online courses have enabled individuals to connect with like-minded people and learn about non-theistic philosophies from around the world. This accessibility has democratized spirituality, allowing people to craft their own spiritual journeys by drawing from a wide range of teachings and practices. The availability of digital resources has accelerated the spread of ideas and movements that are not tied to religious institutions, making it easier for individuals to explore and integrate non-theistic spiritual practices into their lives.

In addition, non-theistic spiritual movements are growing because they offer **flexibility and adaptability** in a rapidly changing world. Traditional religious institutions often have fixed doctrines and rituals that may not resonate with modern individuals who value personal freedom and diversity of thought. Non-theistic movements, on the other hand, allow for greater personalization and adaptability, enabling individuals to explore spirituality in ways that are meaningful to them without feeling confined by rigid structures. Whether through the practice of mindfulness, ethical living, or environmental stewardship, these movements provide individuals with the tools to create a spiritual path that aligns with their unique perspectives, needs, and experiences.

As societies become more **globalized and pluralistic**, non-theistic spiritual movements also appeal to those who seek a more universal and inclusive approach to spirituality. Many of these movements emphasize the shared human experience, focusing on values such as compassion, kindness, and interconnectedness rather than religious divisions or sectarianism. This inclusive approach resonates with individuals who are disillusioned with religious exclusivity and are looking for spiritual practices that unite rather than divide. By promoting ethical living, mindfulness, and personal growth, non-theistic spiritual movements transcend cultural and religious boundaries, offering a form of spirituality that is accessible and relevant to people from all walks of life.

In conclusion, non-theistic spiritual movements are growing worldwide as people increasingly seek spiritual fulfillment outside the confines of traditional religious institutions. These movements offer a more personal, flexible, and inclusive approach to spirituality, focusing on self-awareness, ethical living, mindfulness, and connection to nature. As disillusionment with organized religion continues and people explore new ways of finding meaning, non-theistic movements provide a path for spiritual exploration that aligns with modern values and the complexities of contemporary life. This global trend reflects a deep desire for spirituality that is grounded in personal growth, inner peace, and a sense of connection to the broader world, without the need for belief in the divine.

The increasing focus on self in a secular, globalized world

IN TODAY'S SECULAR, globalized world, there is a growing emphasis on the individual self as the center of meaning, identity, and personal fulfillment. As traditional religious and cultural frameworks evolve or decline, more people are turning inward, focusing on self-discovery, personal development, and self-expression as key aspects of their lives. This increasing focus on the self reflects broader societal changes—such as the rise of individualism, the influence of secularism, and the rapid pace of globalization—which are reshaping how people understand their purpose and navigate their existence in a complex and interconnected world.

One of the primary reasons for the rise in self-focused philosophies and practices is the **shift toward individualism** in many modern societies. In contrast to traditional cultures that emphasized collective identity, duty to family or community, and adherence to religious or social norms, contemporary societies often place a higher value on personal autonomy and self-expression. This shift has led individuals to prioritize their own personal goals, desires, and well-being over societal expectations. As a result, people are more likely to seek fulfillment through the exploration of their own identity, values, and personal growth, rather than relying on external authorities or prescribed roles.

The **secularization** of many parts of the world has also played a significant role in the increasing focus on self. As religious influence declines in various societies, many individuals are moving away from belief systems that provide predefined answers to life's big questions—such as the nature of existence, morality, and purpose. Instead, people are turning to secular philosophies, psychological approaches, and self-help movements that emphasize the individual's responsibility to create their own meaning and define their own values. This secular approach to life fosters a deeper focus on the self as the source of answers to existential questions, rather than seeking guidance from a divine being or religious authority.

In this context, **self-awareness** and **personal growth** have become central themes in the lives of many people. The focus on self-awareness encourages individuals to explore their inner world, reflect on their thoughts, emotions, and behaviors, and seek a deeper understanding of their motivations and desires. Through practices such as mindfulness, journaling, therapy, and meditation, people aim to cultivate greater insight into their true selves and live in alignment with their core values. This inward journey is seen as essential for achieving personal fulfillment, emotional balance, and a sense of purpose in a world where external markers of success—such as career achievements or material wealth—often feel insufficient or fleeting.

The rise of **self-help literature, personal development seminars, and coaching** further reflects the increasing focus on self in a globalized world. These industries, which have grown exponentially in recent decades, provide individuals with tools and strategies for personal growth, success, and well-being. From productivity techniques and goal-setting workshops to emotional intelligence training and spiritual coaching, these resources encourage individuals to take control of their own lives and design their futures. The underlying message in much of this content is that individuals have the power to shape their reality, achieve their dreams, and become their best selves. This message resonates with people who are seeking autonomy and empowerment in a fast-paced, competitive world.

The emphasis on **self-expression** and authenticity is another significant aspect of the modern focus on self. In a globalized world, where people are exposed to diverse cultures, ideas, and lifestyles, there is a greater opportunity and pressure to define one's own identity. Social media and digital platforms have amplified this trend, providing individuals with the tools to craft and share their personal narratives with a global audience. This environment encourages people to explore their unique interests, talents, and passions, and to present an authentic version of themselves to the world. The focus on self-expression is often seen as a way to assert individuality and find meaning in an increasingly interconnected and, at times, homogenized world.

Moreover, the globalized world brings with it **greater complexity and uncertainty**, which has also contributed to the inward turn toward the self. In a world where change is rapid, economic structures are shifting, and technological advancements disrupt traditional industries and ways of life, individuals often face feelings of instability and insecurity. The global marketplace, with its demands for constant innovation, flexibility, and adaptability, can leave people feeling overwhelmed and disconnected from traditional sources of stability, such as family, religion, or community. In response, many people are seeking to anchor themselves in their own inner resources, focusing on personal resilience, emotional intelligence, and self-mastery to navigate these uncertainties.

Mental health awareness has also played a critical role in the increasing focus on the self. As conversations around mental health become more widespread and destigmatized, there is greater recognition of the importance of self-care, emotional well-being, and psychological resilience. This has led individuals to place more emphasis on understanding their own emotional and mental states, seeking therapies or practices that promote healing, growth, and self-compassion. The integration of psychological insights into everyday life has empowered individuals to take charge of their mental health, encouraging them to prioritize self-awareness and emotional balance as foundational elements of a fulfilling life.

While the focus on self has many positive aspects—such as fostering personal growth, autonomy, and self-empowerment—it also presents certain challenges. The emphasis on individualism can sometimes lead to **isolation**, as people may feel disconnected from the collective bonds that traditionally provided a sense of belonging and purpose. The pursuit of self-fulfillment, when taken to extremes, can result in a sense of emptiness or loneliness, as individuals realize that personal success or self-actualization does not necessarily guarantee happiness. Additionally, the relentless focus on self-improvement and achievement can contribute to **burnout**, as individuals may feel pressure to constantly strive for perfection or personal success in a highly competitive environment.

In response to these challenges, many people are exploring how to balance the focus on self with a sense of **interconnectedness** and social responsibility. This has led to the rise of movements that blend personal growth with a commitment to community and the environment, such as eco-spirituality, ethical consumerism, and social entrepreneurship. These movements encourage individuals to use their personal development not only for their own benefit but also for the betterment of society and the planet. By integrating the focus on self with a broader sense of purpose, individuals can cultivate a more holistic approach to life that embraces both personal autonomy and collective responsibility.

In conclusion, the increasing focus on self in a secular, globalized world reflects broader cultural shifts toward individualism, autonomy, and personal growth. As traditional religious and societal structures lose their influence, people are turning inward, seeking meaning, fulfillment, and authenticity through self-awareness, self-expression, and personal development. While this inward focus offers many opportunities for empowerment and transformation, it also presents challenges related to isolation, pressure, and the search for deeper connection. As people continue to navigate these complexities, the balance between self-empowerment and collective responsibility will be essential for fostering both personal fulfillment and a sense of belonging in a rapidly changing world.

Chapter 11: The Future of Spirituality Without God

As society continues to evolve, so too does the concept of spirituality. In recent decades, there has been a notable shift away from traditional, theistic religions toward spiritual practices that emphasize self-development, inner growth, and personal responsibility. With fewer people adhering to established religious frameworks, new forms of spirituality are emerging—ones that focus on the individual's journey toward fulfillment, rather than reliance on a divine being. The future of spirituality seems poised to prioritize personal growth, mental well-being, and ethical living over traditional religious doctrines and deities.

This ongoing transformation raises important questions about what spirituality will look like in the coming years. As the focus on self-awareness and inner growth continues to expand, people are crafting new spiritual practices that align with modern values—particularly those of autonomy, reason, and emotional resilience. Practices such as mindfulness, meditation, and personal development are becoming more central to the spiritual experience, often replacing prayer and worship with introspection, self-discipline, and the pursuit of balance.

These emerging spiritual paths reflect a growing belief that meaning and purpose can be found within oneself, rather than from an external deity. Individuals are taking charge of their own spiritual lives, creating practices that are deeply personal and adaptable to the changing world. The future of spirituality, then, may be less about collective religious experiences and more about the individual's journey toward self-discovery and ethical living.

This chapter explores the evolving nature of spirituality as the focus on self and inner growth continues to reshape how people engage with spiritual practices. It examines how individuals are shaping new paths that prioritize personal development and emotional well-being, and what this means for the future of spirituality in a world that increasingly values independence, personal empowerment, and non-theistic approaches to meaning and fulfillment. As the concept of spirituality broadens, it becomes more inclusive and accessible, offering each person the chance to create a unique, deeply personal connection to themselves and the world around them.

What will spirituality look like as the focus on self and inner growth continues to evolve?

AS THE FOCUS ON SELF and inner growth continues to evolve, the future of spirituality is likely to become even more personalized, flexible, and integrative, blending traditional practices with modern approaches to personal development. Spirituality in the coming years will likely be less about adherence to established doctrines or religious institutions and more about individual exploration, self-discovery, and emotional well-being. As society moves further into a globalized and digital age, spirituality will continue to reflect the growing emphasis on personal growth, self-awareness, and inner fulfillment, shaping a landscape where individuals define their own spiritual paths based on their unique needs, experiences, and values.

One of the key aspects of this evolution will be the increasing **individualization of spiritual practices**. As people move away from organized religion and its prescribed rituals, they are more likely to adopt spiritual practices that resonate with their personal beliefs and lifestyle. This could mean incorporating elements from various traditions, such as meditation, mindfulness, yoga, or breathwork, while also drawing on secular practices like journaling, therapy, or nature-based rituals. In this future landscape, individuals will have the freedom to create their own spiritual frameworks, blending elements that help them connect with their inner selves and navigate the complexities of modern life.

This shift toward personal spirituality will also be characterized by an **emphasis on inner growth and emotional healing**. As more people prioritize mental health and emotional well-being, spirituality will increasingly intersect with psychology and personal development. Practices aimed at fostering self-awareness, emotional resilience, and mindfulness will continue to gain traction as essential components of spiritual growth. Meditation, mindfulness, and self-inquiry, once considered niche or alternative, will become even more central to how individuals pursue spiritual fulfillment. These practices will allow individuals to cultivate greater clarity, emotional balance, and inner peace, all of which are crucial for navigating the fast-paced, often stressful nature of modern life.

Another significant development will be the rise of **experiential spirituality**, where individuals focus on direct, personal experiences of transcendence or inner connection rather than relying on external religious authorities or dogmas. As people seek to deepen their spiritual journeys, they will turn to practices that facilitate transformative experiences, such as silent retreats, immersive meditation programs, or even psychedelic-assisted therapies. These experiences, whether through traditional or modern methods, will provide individuals with the opportunity to connect with a deeper sense of self, access expanded states of consciousness, and gain insights into the nature of reality—all without needing to subscribe to a specific religious belief system. This experiential approach will continue to reshape the spiritual landscape by prioritizing personal transformation over external rituals.

Technology will also play a pivotal role in shaping the future of spirituality as it continues to evolve with the focus on self and inner growth. **Digital spirituality**, in the form of online communities, virtual meditation apps, and even AI-powered spiritual guides, will become more prevalent, offering individuals new ways to explore and deepen their spiritual practices. These digital platforms will allow individuals to access spiritual teachings, participate in group meditations, or engage in personalized self-help content from the comfort of their homes. While this technological integration may seem disconnected from traditional spiritual practices, it will offer individuals greater accessibility and flexibility, allowing them to tailor their spiritual growth to their personal schedules and needs.

At the same time, as people continue to seek inner growth, **ethical living and social consciousness** will become central elements of modern spirituality. Increasingly, spirituality will be linked with ethical practices such as veganism, environmental stewardship, and social justice. Individuals will not only focus on their own personal development but will also seek to align their actions with broader values that promote compassion, sustainability, and equality. This shift toward ethically driven spirituality reflects the growing recognition that personal growth is interconnected with the well-being of others and the planet. Spiritual practices will thus become more integrated with efforts to create a more just and harmonious world, blending personal fulfillment with collective responsibility.

Holistic health and well-being will also continue to play a key role in the evolution of spirituality. Many spiritual seekers will embrace the idea that true spiritual growth cannot be separated from physical and emotional well-being. Practices that integrate the mind, body, and spirit, such as yoga, energy healing, or somatic therapies, will become even more central to how individuals approach their spiritual journeys. This holistic approach emphasizes that personal and spiritual growth involves not only inner reflection but also caring for the body, maintaining emotional health, and nurturing one's connection to nature and the environment. As this holistic view of spirituality expands, individuals will adopt practices that nourish every aspect of their being, creating a more balanced and integrated approach to spiritual development.

The future of spirituality will also likely see a greater focus on **community and connection**, even as the emphasis on self and inner growth continues to evolve. While the individual journey will remain central, people will increasingly seek out communities of like-minded individuals with whom they can share their spiritual experiences, challenges, and insights. These communities may not take the form of traditional religious congregations but will instead be fluid, inclusive, and often digitally connected, bringing together people from diverse backgrounds and spiritual paths. This sense of belonging and connection will be crucial in a world that is often fragmented and isolating, allowing individuals to feel supported as they pursue their inner growth.

Despite the emphasis on personal spirituality, many will continue to explore **existential and philosophical questions**, such as the nature of consciousness, the meaning of life, and the experience of death, in their pursuit of inner growth. Non-theistic spiritual movements, such as secular humanism or mindfulness-based philosophies, will provide frameworks for addressing these profound questions without relying on religious answers. Instead, individuals will look to science, philosophy, and direct personal experiences to guide their understanding of these existential issues, further emphasizing the role of self-awareness and personal inquiry in spiritual exploration.

As spirituality continues to evolve with the focus on self and inner growth, there will be a **blurring of boundaries between secular and spiritual practices**. Many practices once considered purely therapeutic or psychological, such as mindfulness or positive affirmations, will be embraced as part of a broader spiritual toolkit. This integration will allow individuals to approach their inner growth from multiple angles, using both secular and spiritual methods to enhance their well-being. The result will be a more fluid understanding of spirituality, where individuals draw from a wide range of practices and philosophies to create a personal path that aligns with their unique needs and desires.

In conclusion, as the focus on self and inner growth continues to evolve, spirituality will become increasingly personalized, experiential, and integrative. The future of spirituality will prioritize personal transformation, emotional healing, and self-awareness, while also incorporating ethical living, community connection, and technological advancements. Individuals will have the freedom to craft their own spiritual journeys, blending traditional wisdom with modern insights to create a path that aligns with their values and supports their inner growth. As this evolution unfolds, spirituality will continue to offer individuals a powerful framework for navigating the complexities of life, fostering both personal fulfillment and a deeper connection to the world around them.

How people are shaping new spiritual practices that prioritize personal development over the divine

AS SPIRITUALITY CONTINUES to evolve in the modern world, there is a noticeable shift toward practices that focus on personal development, self-awareness, and inner growth, rather than traditional religious devotion to divine beings. These new spiritual practices emphasize the individual's journey toward fulfillment, healing, and self-actualization, reflecting a broader cultural trend toward self-empowerment and autonomy. Rather than relying on divine intervention or established religious doctrines, people are creating spiritual frameworks that prioritize emotional well-being, mental clarity, and ethical living as the key elements of a meaningful life. This approach aligns with contemporary values of self-responsibility, personal growth, and the pursuit of inner peace, reshaping the spiritual landscape in profound ways.

One of the key factors driving this shift is the increasing focus on **self-discovery** and **inner work**. In many new spiritual movements, the emphasis is on understanding one's own thoughts, emotions, and behaviors, with the goal of achieving greater self-awareness and personal transformation. Practices like mindfulness, meditation, journaling, and therapy are seen as essential tools for exploring the inner self and uncovering limiting beliefs, unresolved emotions, or unconscious patterns that may be holding individuals back. This process of self-discovery is not about seeking external validation or divine approval but about fostering a deeper connection with oneself and cultivating personal insight. For many, this inner journey leads to a sense of empowerment and fulfillment that transcends traditional religious paths.

These new spiritual practices also place a strong emphasis on **emotional healing and mental well-being**. As people increasingly recognize the importance of mental health and emotional resilience, they are turning to spiritual practices that support healing and self-compassion. Rather than looking to a higher power to solve their problems or alleviate their suffering, individuals are taking responsibility for their own healing journey. This involves engaging in practices like breathwork, somatic therapy, or energy healing to release stored emotions, process trauma, and restore balance to the mind and body. By focusing on emotional healing as a spiritual practice, individuals can cultivate a sense of inner peace and well-being that enhances their personal growth and self-realization.

In addition to emotional healing, the focus on **mindfulness and presence** has become a central aspect of modern spiritual practices. Mindfulness encourages individuals to be fully present in each moment, observing their thoughts and feelings without judgment or attachment. This practice fosters a sense of inner calm and clarity, allowing individuals to navigate life's challenges with greater ease and resilience. Mindfulness is often framed as a way to connect with one's true self and live more authentically, rather than as a path to divine connection or religious enlightenment. In this sense, mindfulness supports personal development by helping individuals cultivate awareness and self-mastery, which are key components of inner growth.

Another significant trend in the shaping of new spiritual practices is the emphasis on **ethical living and personal integrity**. Many contemporary spiritual movements prioritize living in alignment with one's values, emphasizing that personal development involves not only self-awareness but also how individuals contribute to the world around them. Practices like veganism, minimalism, and eco-conscious living are often seen as extensions of spiritual growth, where the individual's actions reflect their commitment to compassion, sustainability, and ethical responsibility. In this context, spirituality is not about seeking divine favor or following religious commandments, but about embodying one's highest ideals and making choices that promote personal integrity and harmony with others and the planet.

The shift away from traditional religious practices toward personal development is also evident in the rise of **self-help and personal growth movements**, which often incorporate spiritual principles without relying on divine beings or religious structures. Books, workshops, and seminars on personal development frequently draw on concepts like the law of attraction, positive thinking, and visualization—ideas that encourage individuals to harness the power of their own minds to create the lives they desire. These practices are framed as ways to tap into one's inner potential and achieve success, happiness, and fulfillment through self-discipline and focus. The emphasis on personal responsibility and empowerment aligns with the broader trend toward spirituality that prioritizes personal growth over reliance on external forces.

Self-compassion and self-love are also increasingly recognized as spiritual practices in modern movements that prioritize personal development. Traditionally, spirituality has often involved self-sacrifice, penance, or devotion to a higher power, but in these newer approaches, the focus is on nurturing oneself with kindness, acceptance, and care. Practices like affirmations, gratitude exercises, and self-care routines are seen as ways to cultivate a deeper relationship with oneself, promoting emotional healing and inner peace. By encouraging individuals to treat themselves with compassion and understanding, these practices foster self-esteem and resilience, allowing people to approach their personal development journey with greater confidence and joy.

As people shape these new spiritual practices, there is also a growing interest in **embodied spirituality**, where the connection between the mind, body, and spirit is emphasized as integral to personal development. Yoga, tai chi, and other movement-based practices are not just seen as physical exercises but as spiritual disciplines that help individuals cultivate awareness, presence, and balance. Through mindful movement, individuals can develop a deeper understanding of their bodies and emotions, releasing tension and stress while fostering inner peace. This holistic approach to spirituality highlights the importance of integrating all aspects of oneself—physical, emotional, and mental—on the path to personal growth.

Community and shared experiences are also playing a role in the evolution of spiritual practices that prioritize personal development. While the focus is often on individual growth, many people are seeking communities of like-minded individuals with whom they can share their journey. These communities, whether in the form of support groups, spiritual retreats, or online networks, provide a space for individuals to connect, share insights, and support each other's personal development. This sense of community is not necessarily religious in nature but is instead built around the shared goal of personal growth, self-improvement, and mutual support. These connections help individuals feel less isolated in their spiritual journeys and offer a sense of belonging and encouragement as they pursue their inner growth.

Another key feature of these emerging spiritual practices is the **integration of science and spirituality**. As people seek to understand the nature of consciousness, personal growth, and well-being, many are turning to both scientific research and spiritual wisdom to guide their practices. Neuroscience, psychology, and positive psychology have become important sources of insight into how the brain works, how emotions are processed, and how individuals can cultivate happiness and resilience. These findings often intersect with spiritual practices like mindfulness, meditation, and gratitude, creating a bridge between empirical knowledge and spiritual experience. This integration allows individuals to approach personal development with both scientific grounding and spiritual depth.

Ultimately, these new spiritual practices reflect a **shift in priorities**—from seeking divine connection or religious salvation to focusing on personal development, inner peace, and ethical living. People are increasingly taking responsibility for their own growth, viewing their lives as a journey of self-discovery and transformation. As traditional religious frameworks give way to more fluid and personalized approaches, individuals are shaping spiritual practices that resonate with their unique values and experiences, allowing them to grow in ways that feel authentic and meaningful to them. This trend is reshaping the spiritual landscape, creating a more inclusive, flexible, and empowering approach to spirituality that is grounded in personal development and inner fulfillment.

Conclusion – The Journey Within: Embracing Spirituality Without a God

Throughout this exploration of spirituality without divine figures, a common theme has emerged: the self, with all its complexities, is at the heart of the spiritual journey. Across various traditions, philosophies, and modern movements, the focus has shifted away from the worship of gods and deities and toward a deeper connection with one's own mind, body, and ethical principles. From Buddhism's path to enlightenment and Jainism's pursuit of non-violence to modern approaches like secular humanism and personal growth, each chapter has shown how individuals can find meaning, purpose, and fulfillment through self-awareness, mindfulness, and ethical living.

These practices—whether rooted in ancient wisdom or modern secular thought—offer a framework for living a spiritually rich life that does not rely on divine intervention or theistic belief. Instead, they empower individuals to cultivate inner peace, resilience, and moral clarity through personal responsibility and introspection. The emphasis is on mastering the self, navigating life's challenges with grace, and nurturing a sense of connection to the world and to others without turning to external deities for guidance.

For those who seek to incorporate these self-focused spiritual practices into their everyday lives, the path forward is one of mindful awareness, ethical choices, and emotional well-being. Meditation, mindfulness, self-care, and ethical decision-making are practical tools for fostering a deeper sense of purpose and inner harmony. By focusing on what can be controlled—thoughts, actions, and personal development—any individual can embark on a fulfilling spiritual journey that honors their unique experiences and values.

As this book has demonstrated, the journey of self-discovery and spiritual growth is deeply personal and endlessly rewarding. Whether through cultivating compassion, practicing self-discipline, or simply being more present in daily life, spirituality without divine figures offers a path to a more meaningful, intentional existence. It is a reminder that the power to live a deeply spiritual life lies within, and that true fulfillment comes from embracing the journey of self-realization and inner growth.

Bringing It All Together: Summarize the core ideas discussed in the book

THROUGHOUT THIS BOOK, we have explored the diverse ways in which people are rethinking and reshaping spirituality in the modern world, focusing less on divine figures and more on personal growth, self-awareness, and inner peace. As the world becomes increasingly secular, globalized, and individualistic, many are turning inward, crafting spiritual paths that prioritize self-discovery, emotional healing, and ethical living. These emerging spiritual practices reflect a profound shift in how individuals approach the meaning of life, their purpose, and their relationship with the world around them.

A central theme in this book has been the evolution of spirituality from a focus on religious devotion to a more personal and self-directed journey. Individuals are no longer bound by traditional doctrines or institutionalized religions; instead, they are seeking practices that align with their own values, experiences, and needs. This shift has allowed for a much more diverse and inclusive understanding of spirituality, where people are free to explore different practices such as mindfulness, meditation, yoga, and self-reflection without the need for belief in a higher power.

One of the core ideas discussed is the importance of **self-awareness** in modern spirituality. Practices that promote mindfulness and introspection, such as meditation and journaling, allow individuals to better understand their thoughts, emotions, and inner worlds. This journey toward self-awareness is not just about knowing oneself better; it's about creating a life that is in harmony with one's true self, free from the constraints of societal expectations or religious dogma. By fostering self-awareness, individuals can make more conscious choices, improve emotional resilience, and cultivate a deeper sense of fulfillment.

Another significant theme is the role of **emotional healing** in spiritual growth. As people become more aware of the impact of unresolved emotions, past traumas, and negative thought patterns, they are turning to spiritual practices that help facilitate emotional healing. Breathwork, somatic therapy, and energy healing are just a few examples of how people are using spiritual tools to process emotions, release past pain, and restore emotional balance. This healing is essential for personal transformation, allowing individuals to break free from the emotional burdens that hold them back and experience greater peace and well-being.

Self-compassion and **self-love** have also emerged as critical components of the modern spiritual journey. Rather than focusing on external validation or divine approval, many people are learning to treat themselves with kindness, understanding, and care. Practices such as affirmations, gratitude, and self-care rituals are helping individuals build a foundation of self-compassion that supports their emotional health and personal growth. In this context, spirituality becomes a practice of nurturing the self, recognizing that true fulfillment comes from within, not from external sources.

The book also highlights the growing integration of **ethical living** with spirituality. As people seek to align their spiritual practices with their values, many are adopting lifestyles that emphasize compassion, sustainability, and social justice. Whether through veganism, environmental activism, or community service, individuals are finding ways to live ethically in accordance with their spiritual beliefs. This shift reflects the understanding that personal growth and inner peace are not separate from how we treat others or the planet, but are deeply interconnected with our actions in the world.

Another key idea is the rise of **holistic approaches** to spirituality, which emphasize the integration of mind, body, and spirit. Practices like yoga, tai chi, and energy work help individuals develop a deeper connection between their physical well-being and their spiritual growth. By nurturing the body through movement, breath, and relaxation, individuals can enhance their mental clarity, emotional stability, and spiritual awareness. This holistic approach underscores the importance of treating the whole self—mind, body, and spirit—as an interconnected system that must be cared for and balanced in order to achieve lasting inner peace.

Finally, we have explored how **community and connection** play a role in the evolving landscape of spirituality. While the focus of modern spirituality is often on personal development, many people are seeking out communities of like-minded individuals who share their values and goals. These communities, whether online or in-person, offer a sense of support, belonging, and shared purpose, allowing individuals to grow together while remaining committed to their own spiritual journeys. This emphasis on community highlights the importance of connection in spiritual growth, reminding us that while the journey is personal, it is often enriched by the presence and support of others.

In bringing all these ideas together, the book shows how spirituality is becoming a more **personalized, flexible, and integrative** experience. It is no longer confined to traditional religious structures but has expanded into a wide array of practices that prioritize personal development, emotional healing, and ethical living. People are creating spiritual paths that resonate with their unique needs, allowing them to grow, heal, and live authentically in a way that is meaningful to them. This shift in spirituality represents a profound transformation in how we understand the self, our purpose, and our place in the world.

Ultimately, the core message of this book is that spirituality, in its modern form, is about cultivating a deeper relationship with oneself and with the world around us. It is about finding meaning, fulfillment, and peace from within, while also acting in ways that reflect our values and contribute to the greater good. As the focus on self and inner growth continues to evolve, spirituality will remain a powerful tool for personal transformation, helping individuals navigate the complexities of modern life with grace, clarity, and a sense of purpose.

Living a Spiritual Life Without a God: Practical tips on how to incorporate these self-focused spiritual practices into everyday life

LIVING A SPIRITUAL life without belief in a god or divine being is increasingly common as more people turn to personal growth, self-awareness, and inner peace as their guiding principles. Without the need for religious rituals or reliance on divine intervention, these self-focused spiritual practices offer a way to live with intention, balance, and fulfillment. The key to incorporating these practices into everyday life is to make them accessible and meaningful, allowing them to blend seamlessly into daily routines and enhance your sense of well-being. Here are practical tips on how to live a spiritually rich life centered on personal development and mindfulness.

One of the most effective ways to embrace a spiritual life without theism is through **mindfulness**. Mindfulness involves being fully present in the moment, aware of your thoughts, emotions, and surroundings without judgment. You can begin to integrate mindfulness into your day by setting aside just a few minutes each morning or evening to practice. Start by sitting quietly and focusing on your breath, observing any thoughts or feelings that arise. Rather than trying to control or avoid them, simply notice them and let them pass. This practice of non-judgmental awareness can reduce stress, increase self-awareness, and help you navigate daily challenges with more clarity and calm.

To make mindfulness a consistent part of your routine, try incorporating it into ordinary activities. For instance, you can practice mindful eating by slowing down during meals, savoring each bite, and paying attention to the flavors, textures, and sensations. Similarly, you can practice mindful walking, where you focus on the physical sensations of each step and the environment around you. This approach helps you stay grounded and connected to the present moment, bringing a sense of peace and focus to even the most mundane tasks.

Another essential practice in living a spiritual life without a god is **self-reflection**. Regular self-reflection allows you to gain insight into your thoughts, behaviors, and emotions, fostering personal growth and self-understanding. You can incorporate self-reflection into your daily life by setting aside time for journaling. Writing down your thoughts, feelings, and experiences helps you process and make sense of them, offering clarity and a deeper connection to your inner self. You can use prompts such as "What am I feeling right now?" or "What did I learn about myself today?" to guide your reflections. Over time, this practice can reveal patterns in your thoughts and behaviors, helping you make intentional choices that align with your values and goals.

In addition to self-reflection, cultivating **self-compassion** is a vital part of this spiritual approach. Without the belief in divine forgiveness, self-compassion becomes essential for emotional healing and resilience. Practice speaking to yourself with kindness, especially during difficult moments, as you would to a close friend. If you make a mistake or face challenges, rather than criticizing yourself, acknowledge your humanity and offer yourself patience and understanding. Incorporating self-compassion into your daily life helps you foster emotional balance and self-worth, allowing you to move through life's difficulties with greater ease.

Gratitude is another simple yet powerful spiritual practice that can transform your perspective. By focusing on what you appreciate in your life, you shift your mindset from scarcity or dissatisfaction to one of abundance and contentment. A simple way to begin is by keeping a gratitude journal, where you write down three things you are thankful for each day. These could be small moments—like enjoying a cup of tea—or more significant experiences, such as spending time with loved ones. Practicing gratitude regularly can improve your emotional well-being, increase positivity, and help you cultivate a deeper sense of connection to the world around you.

Physical practices like yoga, tai chi, or even walking in nature can also serve as forms of embodied spirituality, helping you connect with your body and the present moment. These practices offer a holistic approach to spirituality by integrating mind, body, and spirit. You can set aside time each day or week for these activities, treating them not just as exercise but as a way to center yourself and foster inner peace. By focusing on your breath and movements, you can create a sense of harmony between your physical and mental states, promoting relaxation and mindfulness. Taking walks in nature can also provide a sense of grounding and connection to the larger world, reminding you of the interconnectedness of all life.

Setting intentions for your day or week is another way to bring spirituality into everyday life. Intentions are different from goals in that they focus more on how you want to show up in the world rather than specific outcomes. For example, you might set an intention to be more patient, compassionate, or mindful throughout the day. By reminding yourself of your intention each morning, you can create a mental framework that guides your actions and helps you stay aligned with your deeper values. This practice encourages you to live with greater purpose and presence, enhancing your overall sense of fulfillment.

Emotional healing is another cornerstone of a self-focused spiritual life. Addressing unresolved emotions and healing past wounds allows you to release the emotional baggage that may be holding you back. You can incorporate emotional healing into your routine by engaging in practices like breathwork, somatic therapy, or guided meditations designed to release stored emotions. These practices help you process difficult feelings, create space for new growth, and restore balance to your emotional state. Over time, engaging in emotional healing practices will foster inner peace and resilience, helping you live a more grounded and spiritually fulfilling life.

Acts of kindness and service are also essential for living a meaningful, spiritually rich life. While personal development is a key focus, contributing to the well-being of others brings a sense of purpose and connection. Look for small ways to be of service, whether it's helping a neighbor, volunteering, or simply offering a kind word to someone in need. These acts remind you of the interconnectedness of life and enhance your sense of empathy and compassion. Incorporating acts of kindness into your daily routine helps you feel more connected to others and gives deeper meaning to your spiritual journey.

Finally, as you shape your self-focused spiritual path, it's essential to remain **open to change and growth**. Spirituality is a dynamic, evolving practice, and what works for you today may not be what you need in the future. Give yourself permission to explore different practices and adapt your spiritual routines as your needs and circumstances change. Stay curious about new ideas, reflect on what resonates most deeply with you, and be willing to let go of practices that no longer serve your growth. By staying flexible and open, you allow your spiritual journey to unfold naturally, guided by your own inner wisdom and personal development.

Living a spiritual life without a god offers you the freedom to create a path that is uniquely your own, centered on self-awareness, personal growth, and emotional well-being. By integrating these practical tips into your daily life, you can cultivate a sense of purpose, balance, and fulfillment that nurtures your spirit and enhances your overall well-being. Whether through mindfulness, self-reflection, gratitude, or acts of kindness, each practice invites you to live with greater presence and authenticity, fostering a deep connection to yourself and the world around you.

Final Reflections on the Journey of Self: The personal significance of spirituality that does not rely on divine figures

SPIRITUALITY THAT IS centered on the self rather than divine figures offers a deeply personal and meaningful path for individuals seeking fulfillment, inner peace, and self-discovery. It represents a shift from traditional, theistic religious structures to a more autonomous and self-guided journey that prioritizes personal growth, emotional healing, and the cultivation of values that resonate deeply within. This journey is not about external worship or adherence to dogma but about tuning in to one's own inner world, understanding the self on a deeper level, and making conscious choices that align with personal truth and integrity.

The significance of this form of spirituality lies in its **empowerment of the individual**. Without reliance on divine beings or religious intermediaries, the responsibility for spiritual growth and meaning-making rests entirely within the individual. This empowers people to take full ownership of their journey, shaping it in a way that aligns with their unique values, needs, and experiences. This self-directed path allows for greater freedom and authenticity, as individuals are free to explore practices and philosophies that resonate with them personally, without being confined by external religious expectations or doctrines.

At the heart of self-focused spirituality is the practice of **self-awareness**. This journey involves a deep dive into understanding one's own thoughts, emotions, and motivations. By engaging in practices such as mindfulness, meditation, and self-reflection, individuals develop a heightened sense of self-awareness, allowing them to better understand their inner workings and navigate life's challenges with clarity and calm. This self-awareness leads to a more intentional and mindful way of living, where decisions are made based on an authentic understanding of one's values and desires. It also fosters greater emotional intelligence, helping individuals manage their emotions and build healthier relationships with others.

Another core aspect of spirituality without divine figures is the focus on **emotional healing and personal transformation**. The journey of self is often one of healing—addressing past wounds, processing unresolved emotions, and learning to let go of pain and limiting beliefs that no longer serve us. This aspect of the journey is about freeing oneself from the emotional baggage that hinders growth and cultivating a sense of inner peace and resilience. By prioritizing healing, individuals are able to move through life with a greater sense of wholeness, letting go of what weighs them down and stepping into a more empowered, authentic version of themselves.

Without the framework of divine beings to provide meaning or purpose, individuals who embrace self-focused spirituality must also engage in **personal meaning-making**. This journey asks individuals to reflect on what gives their life meaning and purpose, and how they want to contribute to the world. For some, meaning might be found in personal relationships, creative expression, or acts of service to others. For others, it might come through a commitment to ethical living, social justice, or environmental stewardship. By crafting a life that is aligned with their personal sense of purpose, individuals can experience deep fulfillment and satisfaction, knowing that their actions and choices reflect their core values.

Interconnectedness also plays a significant role in self-focused spirituality. Even without the belief in a divine entity, many people on this path recognize the interconnectedness of all life. This understanding fosters a sense of compassion and empathy, not just for oneself but for others and the planet. By recognizing that we are all part of a larger whole, individuals can cultivate a sense of responsibility toward others and the environment. This often leads to ethical practices, such as non-violence, sustainability, and kindness, which are seen as extensions of one's personal spiritual growth. The journey of self, therefore, is not isolated or self-centered but deeply connected to the well-being of others and the world.

The **fluidity and adaptability** of this spiritual path is another significant aspect. Unlike traditional religious paths that often require adherence to specific rituals, beliefs, or practices, self-focused spirituality is highly flexible. It evolves with the individual, adapting to changing circumstances, needs, and insights. This fluidity allows for a more personalized experience, where individuals can experiment with different practices—such as meditation, journaling, yoga, or creative expression—to see what resonates with them at any given time. This adaptability ensures that spirituality remains relevant and meaningful, supporting individuals through various stages of life and personal growth.

In addition, spirituality that does not rely on divine figures places a strong emphasis on **self-compassion** and **self-acceptance**. Without the need for divine forgiveness or external validation, individuals learn to cultivate compassion for themselves, acknowledging their imperfections, struggles, and growth with kindness. This self-compassion is essential for emotional well-being and resilience, allowing individuals to move through challenges with greater ease and confidence. By practicing self-compassion, individuals learn to embrace themselves fully, finding peace in who they are rather than striving for an unattainable ideal of perfection.

The journey of self-focused spirituality is ultimately one of **inner freedom**. It frees individuals from the constraints of external religious authority, enabling them to explore and express their spirituality in ways that feel authentic and meaningful to them. This freedom fosters a sense of autonomy and personal power, as individuals realize that they have everything they need within themselves to create a life of meaning, purpose, and peace. This form of spirituality encourages individuals to trust their inner wisdom, take responsibility for their own growth, and embrace the beauty of the journey, regardless of external circumstances.

In conclusion, the personal significance of spirituality that does not rely on divine figures lies in its deep connection to self-empowerment, emotional healing, and inner growth. This path allows individuals to craft a spiritual journey that is authentic, flexible, and deeply aligned with their personal values and experiences. It emphasizes the importance of self-awareness, self-compassion, and interconnectedness, helping individuals cultivate a sense of inner peace and fulfillment. As people continue to explore these self-focused spiritual practices, they are finding new ways to live with intention, balance, and purpose, creating a life that is meaningful, grounded, and enriched by personal growth.

Appendix

This section provides additional resources, references, and practical exercises to support readers on their journey of self-focused spirituality. The appendix aims to offer tools that can help deepen your understanding of the practices discussed throughout the book, while giving you guidance on how to incorporate them into your daily life.

1. Recommended Books and Resources

- *The Power of Now* by Eckhart Tolle: A foundational book on mindfulness and living in the present moment.

- *The Untethered Soul* by Michael A. Singer: Focuses on spiritual awakening and emotional freedom.

- *Radical Acceptance* by Tara Brach: A guide to self-compassion and emotional healing.

- *Wherever You Go, There You Are* by Jon Kabat-Zinn: A practical introduction to mindfulness meditation.

- *Man's Search for Meaning* by Viktor Frankl: An exploration of meaning-making in life, even through suffering.

2. Suggested Meditation Techniques

- **Breathing Meditation**: Find a quiet space, sit comfortably, and focus on your breath. Observe each inhale and exhale without judgment. If your mind wanders, gently bring your attention back to your breath.

- **Body Scan Meditation**: Lie down and close your eyes. Bring awareness to different parts of your body, starting at your toes and moving upwards. Notice sensations without trying to change anything.

- **Loving-Kindness Meditation**: Sit quietly and focus on cultivating feelings of compassion and love. Silently repeat phrases such as "May I be happy, may I be well, may I be peaceful." Extend these thoughts to others, including loved ones, acquaintances, and even difficult people.

3. Gratitude Journaling Prompts

- What three things am I most grateful for today?

- Who in my life has made a positive impact on me recently, and how can I show them gratitude?

- What small moment from today brought me joy or comfort?

4. Self-Reflection Questions

- What are my core values, and how do I align my daily actions with them?

- When do I feel most connected to myself? How can I create more of these moments in my life?

- What emotions am I currently holding onto, and what steps can I take to heal and release them?

5. Practical Ways to Practice Mindfulness

- **Mindful Eating**: Slow down and savor each bite. Pay attention to the flavors, textures, and smells of your food.

- **Mindful Walking**: While walking, focus on the sensation of your feet touching the ground and the rhythm of your steps. Notice the sights and sounds around you.

- **Mindful Listening**: When in conversation, give your full attention to the other person without thinking about how you'll respond. Be present and open.

6. Daily Affirmations for Self-Compassion and Growth

- "I am worthy of love and respect."
- "I embrace the process of growth and learning."
- "I forgive myself for past mistakes and focus on the present."
- "I trust my inner wisdom to guide me through life."

7. Online Communities and Support Groups

- Insight Timer: A meditation app with a global community offering guided meditations, courses, and groups.

- Mindful.org: An online resource for articles, guided practices, and mindfulness-based courses.

- Meetup: Search for local or virtual groups centered on meditation, mindfulness, yoga, or personal growth.

8. Ethical Living and Sustainability Resources

- *The Minimalists*: A website and podcast focused on simplifying life and living with intention.

- *Becoming Minimalist* by Joshua Becker: A blog that explores minimalism and decluttering.

- *Earth Hero*: An online resource for sustainable living practices and products.